PRAISE FOR "POSITIVELY ALTERED"

"If you thought cancer could not possibly be funny, Dr. Cindy Howard's book will change your view. For her, laughter is a wellness strategy, one of a wide array of healing tools she employed to strengthen her mind and body through months of chemotherapy. Her cancer story is a lively and engaging read—raw, honest, and often hilarious.

"It feels like listening to a very amusing friend talk about her life late into the night after a good dinner; she's letting everything hang out, whether admirable, irritating, embarrassing, sad, or funny. You'll have moments where you go 'Ow!' or 'Eeeww' or 'Seriously, you did what?!' And in between the funny bits and the angry bits, she drops in some interesting wellness information and some provocative opinions.

"For anyone facing a life challenge, this book makes a persuasive case that, in addition to seeking out medical expertise, it's vital to know yourself and harness that self-knowledge to promote healing."

—Edith Forbes, author of *Alma Rose, Nowle's Passing*, and *Tracking a Shadow*

"I couldn't put this one down; it made me laugh, and it made me cry. Cindy's story is a wonderful example of how to smile in the face of adversity, to say 'Try me!' instead of 'Why me?' and to have the faith to stay 'in spirit' through the toughest of times. Cindy is David and has slayed Goliath!"

—Bill Storm, corporate trainer, international speaker, Tony Robbins Companies

"Pull up a chair, grab a glass of wine or a cup of coffee, and enjoy this conversation with Dr. Howard. You'll be drawn in by her breezy banter, positive outlook, and unabashed honesty. With asides galore, *Positively Altered* is like sitting down with your best girlfriend and dishing on some of life's most difficult challenges—cancer, divorce, child-rearing."

—Renée Harmon, MD, author of
Surfing the Waves of Alzheimer's

"Cindy is the perfect person to write a book about making room for what's important in your life. When you leave a conversation with her, you can't help but feel inspired to move the needle a little further in a positive direction. With a caring personality, confidence, and an unapologetic drive, Cindy brings out the best in all of us. She shows up on each page of her book with vulnerability and empathy for the various challenges we face."

—Stephanie Halloran, chiropractic
physician, Boundless Health

"Do yourself a favor; don't drink any liquids while reading this memoir, or you might find them coming out of your nose! Cindy's hilarious delivery on topics ranging from relationships to raising kids to navigating cancer is not to be missed. Her unique and optimistic outlook will challenge you to think differently about your own life and any adversity you're facing. Refreshingly and sometimes shockingly real, Cindy's personal obstacles become your learning opportunities."

—Joey Coleman, award-winning keynote speaker
and author of *Never Lose an Employee Again* and
Never Lose a Customer Again

POSITIVELY ALTERED

POSITIVELY

Finding Happiness at the Bottom of a Chemo Bag

ALTERED

DR. CINDY M. HOWARD

Flamingo Press

Author's Note: You may notice that I write the word *G-d* instead of using an *o* in the hyphen's place. This is a Jewish custom, and many believe it is a sign of respect. The idea is that you avoid writing G-d's name so that the word is never unintentionally destroyed or thrown away.

Excerpt on page 45 from *Breaking the Habit of Being Yourself*, by Joe Dispenza, copyright 2012, published by Hay House, Inc., Carlsbad, CA, and reprinted with permission from Hay House.

Published by Flamingo Press
www.drcindyspeaks.com

Cover design: Tony Steck, creative director
Project management: Mari Kesselring
Image credits: Tony Steck, DOXA/VANTAGE

ISBN (hardcover): 979-8-9877093-0-6
ISBN (paperback): 979-8-9877093-1-3
ISBN (ebook): 979-8-9877093-2-0
ISBN (audiobook): 979-8-9877093-3-7

Library of Congress Control Number: 2023906839

To my mother, who didn't believe complaining was an option, who would answer, "Cured" when asked how she was, and who believed, "It is what it is." She comes back to me as a pink flamingo just like she decided, because her earthly body is now at rest and truly pain-free.

For the strength and humor and sarcasm and love, I am eternally grateful.

AUTHOR'S DISCLAIMER

The content of this book is for entertainment and informational purposes only and is not intended to diagnose, treat, cure, or prevent any condition or disease. It is intended to shake you up, make you laugh, and push you. The words reflect my feelings, opinions, and observations. I expect you will agree with some things and disagree with others. Some sections might even upset you, and if that happens, I suggest that you learn something about yourself to understand why you feel that way. This was my journey, and I do not want to change anything, even if my words unintentionally offend. Please understand that this book is not intended as a substitute for consultation with a licensed practitioner; you might be going through hard times, but you haven't lost your common sense. Please consult with your own physician or healthcare specialist regarding the suggestions and recommendations that worked for me or that have helped my patients.

XO,

Cindy, a.k.a. Dr. Cindy M. Howard,
DC, DABCI, DACBN, FIAMA, FICC

CONTENTS

Foreword xiii

Preface: Potato Salad xvii

1: My New Favorite Day 1

2: "I Want to Write a Book" 11

3: Winning! 15

4: Pay Attention 21

5: Boys Don't Like Shopping for Panties 29

6: Cindy's Food and Poop Rules 33

7: "Booby" Can Be a Big Word 43

8: The Characters in Your Cancer Story 49

9: If the Guitar Center Sells Guitars,

    What's the Cancer Center Selling? 55

10: Cancer Connect-the-Dots 67

11: Do Something New 77

12: The Two-Martini Accident 85

13: My First Cancer Friend 99

14: Why I Got Divorced During Chemotherapy 105

15: Fifty-One Things I Want in a Man 115

16: The Duplex Theory 123

17: Tony Makes Me Radioactive 129

18: Hope Is a Choice 135

19: Not Great 139

20: I Decide What Hair I Lose 145

21: She Said a Lot of People Don't Like Me 157

22: Giving Up 165

23: How to Miss a Day of Work 173

24: The Curiosity 179

25: Medicine Sucks, and We Take Our Hands for Granted . . 181

26: Conversations with Dr. Block 187

27: Excuses 191

28: Maybe Cancer Will Help 193

29: Last Day of Treatment 197

30: The Cancer Didn't Kill Me, but the Air Might 199

31: Top-Ten Lists 205

32: Barbados 207

33: Happy Chinese Takeout Day 209

34: Premier Passenger 213

Postscript: Valentine's Day 217

Post-Postscript: Six Years Later 219

Last Postscript, I Promise: The Story of My Ghostwriter . . 231

Acknowledgments 235

About the Author 241

FOREWORD

In December 2015, I traveled to Chicago to take one of my first courses in the diplomate program in diagnosis and internal disorders. During this particular weekend, we learned about laboratory testing, and basic urinalysis was our first topic. For those of you not in the medical field, this is the test where you pee in a cup.

As part of the learning experience, we were all sent to the bathroom to, well, run our own tests. When we returned from the bathroom, the instructor said, "You know what would be fun? If we took a picture with our pee cups. Well, that would probably be weird, but I'm weird, so we're going to do it! Everyone hold up your pee and smile!" That was the first time I met Dr. Cindy Howard.

Over the last several years, Cindy has become a great mentor of mine. When she asked me to read this manuscript, I couldn't say no, though I probably should have. I was experiencing a lot of big life changes and had just moved to a new state, started a new job, and started the dating process (again), and I was about to leave for a three-week trip to Africa. I felt like I was flying by the seat of my pants for those nine months leading up to my flight to Doha. By the time I returned from my trip, I had only two days to finish the book and provide feedback before her deadline.

It's hard to believe that a person could benefit from any more inspiration immediately after climbing Mount Kilimanjaro, but this book delivered just that. Coming back from my adventure, I felt refreshed and clearheaded. I was never more in tune with my wants and needs for the present and the future. I had long neglected back-burner projects that were important to me, and they kept getting pushed out of the way for commitments that I felt less passionate about. Cindy's message gave me the nudge I needed to focus on what brought me the most joy; the rest would work out the way the universe intended.

Cindy is the perfect person to write a book about making room for what's important in your life. When you leave a conversation with her, you can't help but feel inspired to move the needle a little further in a positive direction. With a caring personality, confidence, and an unapologetic drive, Cindy brings out the best in all of us. She shows up on each page of her book with vulnerability and empathy for the various challenges we face.

She represents the doctor who is sick, the entrepreneur who hits an unexpected obstacle, the mother who is scared, and the divorcée who is both celebrating and mourning the changes in an intimate relationship. That's why this book is for everyone. She has a way of making you feel seen and heard with her honesty and straightforward personality.

Cindy provides a space to recognize the significant impact an experience may have on you while acknowledging the need for intrinsic motivation to move through it in a positive way. It is a valuable lesson for every reader: the ability to approach and overcome challenges, reframe the way you see your missteps, and create a life that you love where you can find joy.

It's difficult to show up for yourself and honor your own needs, particularly in a world where we're constantly told how we can make ourselves valuable or what we're supposed to do—and even more so with the high level of shame that can occur around personal choices and boundaries.

It's also a challenge to admit when you thought something would work but it didn't and you need to pivot or you'll be at risk of prolonging something in fear of letting others down. I think this is something that most people struggle with throughout their lives. It takes a very strong person with a high level of self-worth to be as vulnerable as Cindy is in this book. The path she took through cancer (and life) is uncommon, but she did it exactly the way she wanted, and she owned it, which she demonstrates on every page.

The world would be an exponentially better place if we all showed up in life with Cindy's curiosity, unrelenting spirit, and approach to making every day more beautiful than the last. I hope that this book provides you with a transformational call to action and that Cindy is as impactful in your life as she has been in mine.

—Stephanie Halloran
Chiropractic Physician
Masters in Functional Medicine and Nutrition
Boundless Health

PREFACE: POTATO SALAD

Should potato salad come in more than one variety?

I mean, potato salad *does* come in more than one variety; there is more than one way to make it. I found an article on FoodNetwork. com that had fifty recipes for potato salad, including one with pickles, one with bacon (no thanks; I actually don't care for it), and one with chicken. If you ask me, that last one prompts the question, When does a potato salad become a chicken salad?

That's not the real question, though. The real question for me is, How do *I* make a potato salad?

My friend Kris got me thinking about potato salad when we first met at a big chiropractic conference in Florida. I present there regularly. I have a board certification in internal medicine and nutrition, and I practice as a primary care provider. Due to my specialty, I am invited to sit on a variety of panels to share my expertise through case studies. Kris came to speak as well. We instantly clicked, so she gave me her phone number right after our presentation together. I make new friends all the time, but I quickly knew that this one was very like-minded, in business and in life. Over the next thirty-six hours, we spoke on two more panels together, shared meals, had a couple drinks, and held up an elevator on the third floor of the hotel because we didn't want to stop our conversation.

Kris mentioned the idea of having a *why* in your practice. I, too, have always emphasized the *why* when speaking with patients or with my consulting clients. (Thank you, Simon Sinek. Love your book *Start with Why: How Great Leaders Inspire Everyone to Take Action!*) Whether you are in business to sell hammers or starting up a new software company or helping people with their physical health, you need to have a *why*. A *why* you are creating something, a *why* you are interested and interest*ing*, a *why* what you have meets some need of your client or end user, and a *why* that creates success. Many people understand who they are and what they do, but they have trouble explaining why a customer should connect with them over someone else doing a similar thing.

To illustrate, Kris said, "Imagine you were invited to a picnic, and everyone brought only potato salad. It would not just be boring, but we'd all quickly get sick of potato salad." Her point was that we should all bring something unique to the picnic. Let people choose what they want from a variety of great but distinct options.

My mind went to a different place, though. As soon as she said that everyone brought potato salad, I thought, *Yeah, but I would make mine from sweet potatoes. I've never made a potato salad with sweet potatoes, but I'll be damned if I'm bringing the same salad as everyone else to your picnic.* Before Kris had even made her point about being unique, I had already imagined things my own way. When I thought about it, I realized I had picked a healthier choice too. I chose something unexpected but also good for you.

That's very on-brand for me. I've learned over time that I think differently from a lot of people, and I'm not afraid to be the oddball

in the room. I love to ponder and wonder why we do things the way
we do. Like, who made the rule that said we had to make potato salad
just this way or that way? Or how chicken can go in a potato salad
and it's still potato salad.

Or (and bear with me now), why does *cancer* have to be a big,
bad, scary word? Or rather, why is it that once you tell people you
have cancer, it's supposed to be the defining fact of your life?

Don't get me wrong: Cancer sucks. More than almost anything
else I've been through. Except pregnancy. And maybe my divorce.

And I also know that not everyone's cancer journey is or can be
the same. This is my story, and while I believe others can benefit from
it and even imitate parts of it, it won't be for everyone. I'm okay with
that.

The big point is that when I learned I had cancer, I refused to
let it be the main fact of my life, the thing that defined who I was.
Hodgkin's lymphoma has a pretty good cure rate, so knowing that
helped. But I didn't want everyone to always be thinking, *There
goes Cindy. She has cancer.* Besides not being the thing I want to be
remembered for, it's kind of a conversation killer, and if you know me,
you know I hate to kill a good conversation.

I wrote the core of this book as a series of journal entries during
six months of treatment in the first half of 2014. I have had time to
go back and get some perspective on that period. I've revised some
entries to reflect that, and I've added new essays that comment on
different parts of my life, but there's still a lot in here that represents
my raw, in-the-moment experience, which may not always be
socially acceptable or entirely coherent. But that's me. I'm not into
sugarcoating or polishing a cancer story any more than I'm into
bemoaning my fate and making everyone feel sorry for me.

I believe we should be honest about who we are but also that we
can choose what we believe about ourselves. Does that make sense?

Maybe it doesn't. Let me put it this way: Though this book is about my cancer journey, my cancer isn't the point of the book. Cancer was just the test for something I've always believed—that is, that we get to choose how we approach our lives, how we react to what the universe throws at us.

We can let cancer overwhelm us and define us and make us miserable and defeated, or we can choose to live our best lives even while getting pumped full of poisonous chemotherapy once a week. We can choose to give in to the depression and anxiety that threaten to overwhelm us at every step, or we can choose to hold on to the belief that we are strong and powerful and capable of coming out on the other end of this crap as the same or even a better person than we went in as.

So, yes, this book has a cancer story, but it's really about making cancer only part of the story. It's about a Jewish girl in a shitty marriage who has a Wonder Woman complex, who had to learn to accept help from the personal Justice League that came together right when she needed them. It's about having some great adventures and finding joy on some days and then feeling sick and depleted on others. It's about having cancer my own way, not the way everyone thought I was supposed to have it.

I do hope you like my potato salad, meaning this quirky, vulnerable, patchwork quilt of a book. I hope it inspires you. I hope it makes you laugh or at least roll your eyes. I want you to think differently too. What kind of potato salad would you bring? I want you to walk through life with an attitude that always brings you gifts and makes you smile.

When I speak professionally, which I've been doing now for over fifteen years, I say at the beginning of my presentation that it is my job to provide you with at least one clinical pearl or one useful insight that you can use when you get back to the office. "Actually," I say, "I would love it if I gave you something you can use before you leave the room. If I can do that, then I have done *my* job. If I haven't, that's on *you*." This usually gets people's attention. I tell them that if they haven't learned something useful, then it's on them to ask at least one question of me to fix that.

The same is true here. If you get something—a giggle, a new perspective, some extra paper to throw in the fireplace when you are done reading—then my stories and musings will have served their purpose. If not, then I hope you'll dig a little deeper and see if something, anything in here doesn't help you see the world a little differently than you did before. Maybe it will just help you see into the mind of someone who thinks differently than you.

Or send me an email with your question, and I'll try to make it up to you that way. Oh, wait. I hate email. Okay, email me, but know that I get buried under emails and am often far behind on replying. Then send an email saying you sent me an email and pray to the junk-mail fairies it doesn't wind up there. You should also consider smoke signals and carrier pigeons or stalking me in Chicago. (But, seriously, don't stalk me.)

Silliness aside, I am honored to share these anecdotes and reflections with you. They are close to my heart. Share them or burn them, knowing that.

Happy reading.

1

MY New FAVORiTe DAY

I have often told people that January 2 is my favorite day of the year. "I hate the holidays," I say. "I can't wait until January second when they are over and done with and I can get back to my life."

But I've said lots of things over the years. Things I think sound funny or smart. Sometimes they're one or the other or both. Sometimes they turn out to be neither.

I used to threaten to leave town before Thanksgiving and not return until January 2. Just skip all the fourth-quarter holidays and New Year's Day. I said I would go somewhere they don't celebrate American holidays. I would find a beach and lie out all day with a hot foreigner on hand. The one I have in mind doesn't speak English but understands it, so he can bring me a mai tai whenever I ask for one.

Funny thing is, I don't even drink mai tais. I am a whiskey girl. Black Label on the rocks—'cause that, usually, is all the bar or restaurant has. Really, I would prefer Blue Label. If you can afford it, that is—I don't buy my own drinks (just ask my friend Jay).

So, my mai tai vacation doesn't make sense because I don't drink mai tais. My January 2 fascination isn't much better. What is January 2 but the beginning of another countdown to more holidays?

Well, I've arrived at a solution of sorts. In 2013, I picked a new favorite day: December 21. That was when I diagnosed myself with cancer. The normal thing to do might be to say it was the worst day of my life, but I wasn't going to do that. I wanted to change my perspective, so I chose it as my new favorite day.

That afternoon, I was treating a patient who had an abnormal Pap smear. She told me her mother had stage 4 ovarian cancer. That was a family having some bad times. I was still thinking about her when I got the fax of the CT report I had ordered for my own neck and chest. I saw words I had only ever seen on patient reports, words that never used to refer to *me* as the patient: *Lymphoma, metastatic or other neoplastic disease.*

Shit.

I guess I should back up. Three weeks prior, I noticed a lump on the left side of my neck. Before I could clearly discern that it was a lump, I'd thought my neck was getting fatter, which was weird because I had been training a lot. And by training, I mean working with my bodybuilder friend Lori with the goal of doing a physique show. I've always been a workout nut. I was big into the world of weight lifting in my twenties. For a while, I even held the Illinois state records for bench press and dead lift for my weight class. All natural, of course. When I met Lori at the gym, I thought it would be fun to try my hand at something a little different.

So there we were, doing ninety minutes of cardio at a time and lifting a ton, and it was great. But while Lori got really lean, I was getting fatter. Then I saw the lump.

It was moveable and non-tender until I started to poke the shit out of it (now I've used that word twice, and this book is just getting started, but I have a feeling it's going to be that kind of process). Then it became sore. My mother had a history of hypothyroidism, so that was where my mind went first and why I ordered the blood work.

Let me back up again. A couple years before all this, my mom started feeling unwell. The working diagnosis was irritable bowel syndrome because she had unexplained diarrhea, but I wasn't buying it. They had her doing blood tests and stool tests, and they weren't coming up with anything really useful. One day, I remember I was driving east on I-80/I-90 toward Indiana when she called, and she was telling me how awful she'd been feeling and how she had lost thirty pounds really fast, and I had to pull off the highway into a hotel parking lot to process what I'd just heard.

When someone loses that much weight without trying, it's Medicine 101 to rule out cancer first. Sometimes it doesn't show up in the tests—sometimes in medicine, you can't diagnose something until it's ready to be found. But sometimes, as a physician, you have an instinct. Somehow, right then, I knew, just knew. My eyes teared up, and I said, "Mom, I'm going to tell you something. I don't know exactly what's wrong with you, but I'm going to tell you right now, you have cancer, and nobody's found it yet."

It was a sobering moment, but it put us on the road to finding what was really wrong with her. On July 4, 2013, she got the confirmation, not the type of fireworks you would expect: multiple myeloma and amyloidosis. Basically, the first one goes after your bone marrow; the second goes after your organs. They're scary, though you can sometimes live a long time with multiple myeloma. But what my mom had, you don't recover from.

The diagnosis came more than two years after the onset of her symptoms. Mom had too many doctors and visits at this point to keep count of. She hired and fired many who did not give her answers or, more disturbingly, stopped looking. You have to keep looking for your patients. Mom struggled daily with eating enough calories because high-calorie foods aren't usually healthy foods. So I would encourage more quantity to get her calories, and my dad would pick her up a donut, a milkshake, or a Big Mac (yuck).

All this was in the back of my mind when I ordered the CT.

Of course, I'm such an idiot—I looked at the results between patients. I wanted to know so that I didn't obsess over them all day, but then I read them and wound up fighting not to obsess over them all day. I had about thirty seconds to process the results, and then I realized, *Oh, no. There's a patient in the other room who needs my attention. I just learned I have cancer, but this moment can't be all about me.* It's always about the patient in my office, never me; I needed to get my shit together and do my job.

Normal people go through their primary care physician for this kind of thing. We physicians, though, think we know better because we deal with this stuff every day—as if we can be as objective and professional about ourselves as we are with our patients.

It's a control thing. The scariest part about running tests is that in-between time when you know something's wrong, but you don't know what it is. I didn't want to go through the rigmarole where you wait for days to get a call from the doctor, but when he finally does call, you miss the call; then he has to leave a message and you try to call him back, and you spend a whole day missing each other, so it's in the back of your mind for way too many hours.

The flip side is that once you get your results, you're sitting alone in a room thinking, *Okay, now what?* You suddenly wish you had your doctor there to tell you it's going to be okay and here's what we're going to do next.

Instead, you feel suddenly very alone, and you realize you still have four more patients to see today. Now, you are the only person in the world who bears the burden of this knowledge. It's simultaneously this very intimate information and something you want to share with someone; it's too much to carry alone.

When I reread my journal from that day, I remember what it was like.

December 21, 2013

My shoulders. Lately they've been getting crowded out by my neck.

Here's the thing: This mass sticks out of the left side of my neck, and yes, if you look, you can see it.

It's a bit like one of Frankenstein's bolts except it is round like a ball instead of cylindrical. Each morning I stare at it in the mirror, trying not to imagine some tiny alien bursting out of it or something weird oozing out. Allowing my imagination to go down whatever grotesque rabbit hole it wants is a thing I do when I don't know what else to do because I don't have control of a situation.

Like, what if I had one on the right side to match? Then at least I could get them pierced and hang earrings on them. That would be fun, since sometimes I can't decide which earrings I am in the mood for, and this would mean I wouldn't have to decide. But, let's face it: if I had to pick two pairs of earrings, I'd still be indecisive. Should they match each other or just my outfit? Should they decorate my lumps or disguise them? Are neck earrings even appropriate before 9:00 p.m.?

But I am asymmetrical. All my masses are on

the left side. Yes, all of them. Two more showed up later; I guess they got stuck in traffic. I am currently working on names for them. I want to acknowledge them after all, these guests, these ride-alongs. I also want to be able to address them properly when I write their Dear John letters after this is all over. (I never did give them a first name, or a middle name, or even a really great nickname.)

Okay, so back to my dilemma. The mass on one side might actually work out for the best. Here is what I am thinking: I have two piercings in my left ear and three in my right, so now, if I pierce the mass, it will even things out. Yes, I'm still on the earring thing. What dilemma did you think I meant?

In high school, it was cool to have uneven piercings. Most girls went all the way up the cartilage, but I was too chicken for that. Now that I am almost forty-five, the asymmetry is not as cool, and I usually don't even put earrings in the second and third holes. Still, with . . . Amanda? Lurch? whatever . . . down there, I'm sure there have been worse excuses for extravagant purchases of diamond stud earrings.

Really, though, today is my new favorite day because it is the day on which I declare I am powerful.

I am brave.

I am strong.

I am funny and I am sexy and I am well, and if I am honest . . .

I am scared shitless.

The scared comes from not knowing exactly what I have or how I am going to attack this, though I know I will attack it with every ounce of my being. And I know I won't be alone; I'll bring a few people along on the journey with me. Or so I hope. Maybe the people who are with me at the end will be different from the people who are with me now, but I believe I will not be alone. I have two people whom I want close to me, whom I want available whenever I need them and even if I don't. They know who they are.

Today is the day I discovered I have cancer. I will face my fears as well as I can and will choose to control what I can control and let the rest go.

I will not use the word can't except right now to acknowledge that I won't use it. Don't ever expect me to give up the word shit because I like it, and I think I'm allowed some freedom of speech and choice here, don't you?

Even from the vantage point of today, when it feels like everything is about to change, 2013 was an amazing year. It shouldn't have been, on paper.

I've had the gift of time to spend with my mother, who is terminal. I am divorcing my husband because I am ready to soar and staying holds me back. I am teaching my boys to be gentlemen and my daughter to be a strong lady. I am valuing the relationship I have with my father. I am really good with my mom, as we both now have had the opportunity to realize life can be short, and it is important to say what you want before you don't have the chance. I have found a new best friend who understands loyalty, trust, unconditional support, and love, and I have my friend Spencer in my life, who understands passion, strength, ambition, and the drive to overachieve, all of which I truly cherish and appreciate. I have some amazing business opportunities that I have been working hard to take advantage of.

Cancer, dying, divorce. Oh, and the dog died. That could be the title of my book. It completes the list, and, I've got to say, I find it really funny at the moment. Funny-absurd, not funny-ha-ha. Like, funny that life or the universe or death or chaos or whatever can be endlessly creative but also endlessly banal. Or plain stupid.

It should all add up to my being a depressed, hopeless heap of human debris. I probably look delusional to people. I'm sure they think I'm in denial. Oh well, what can I do? I really believe there is an upside to everything. And although, today, I have decided that I don't like that phrase that I have been using all year, the phrase is true: This is a gift. A gift to show myself how strong I am and how powerful I can be over what is just another obstacle. I've faced obstacles before. I will hurdle over this one with grace like I have the others. Should I stumble and fall, occasionally, as surely one might when fighting something like this, then I will laugh at myself first and then pick myself up.

I have forty-three minutes until tomorrow, which will mark Day Two of my journey. What

*exciting challenge will come my way? Bring it! I am
ready. I am armed with a mind and determination
to do anything. And I'm not afraid to cry; tears are
how the fear leaks out.*

*There is a one-woman show in this, somewhere.
I will create it every day until I am 112. I have
always said I will live until 112. I might be incoher-
ent and suffering from Alzheimer's when taking the
stage at 112 to tell my story, but if there is one thing
I am sure of, it's that I will still be funny, and I will
still be present, on some level, every day to see the
beauty in the people and the things that surround
me. Tomorrow, the sun will rise, and I will take note
of the colors as I have done a hundred times before,
and I think they will appear brighter and, I hope,
with a bit of orange.*

That's my favorite color.

*This is my journey, and today is my new favor-
ite day, and this next year is going to be fabulous.*

2

"I WANT TO WRITE A BOOK"

(YOU ARE READING IT, A DREAM COME TRUE)

For years, I wanted to write a book. I secretly had this dream of writing an amazing novel that no woman could put down, and it would make men jealous because they'd be asking their wives and girlfriends or partners for sex, only to be told they were too into their book right now.

I mean, how cool would that be? Imagine creating something that grabs someone so powerfully that they would rather sit there with your thing than do anything else. It's influence, sure, but it's also a kind of intimacy, a kind of connection. If we can connect with even just a few people in this life, that's really valuable.

My better-than-sex novel is total nonsense, of course, mostly because I'm not a novelist. What is not nonsense is the kids' health picture book I actually wrote. It was about how the cool kids eat carrots and all the reasons why they do. I wrote it, but it's sitting in a journal waiting for me to find someone who can create beautiful illustrations for it. I also secretly hope that one of my own kids will grow up to be that illustrator, and it will be a joint venture that we all are proud of. Big plans!

Of course, a lot of the things my kids draw would not be appropriate for a kids' book. Sometimes I find a penis traced in the dirt on my car or scribbled on the drawing wall in the basement. Maybe it's best I leave my kids out of this. . . .

But I have another big problem: I can't find the book. I know I wrote the whole story in a black journal, and I swore I knew where I stored it, but after chemo brain (which really happens) and perimenopause (which you have to experience to understand), it is lost somewhere in the wilds of my home. Truth is, my ex probably threw it out like so many other things he got rid of. That's how his mind works; if it isn't his, he tosses it. One good turn deserves another, which is why I eventually threw him out, but now the cool kids will never eat carrots, and no one will know why they were going to.

My own kids will have to be the cool kids now, and I will make it my mission to make sure the cool kids never eat a Lunchables. So far, so . . . well, good enough.

I accepted another challenge instead, without hesitation and with excitement: a story (or journal or book or comedy, I don't know)—my story, about my journey, the one that started December 21, 2013, when I discovered I could be strong and brave in the face of terror. It started as a journal, written one uncertain day at a time. As early as two days after I found out I had cancer, about a week before New Year's 2014, I made my resolution:

December 23, 2013

> *One day, it will be the story of how I kept my head and did the work and got well.*

I hope it's mostly comedy, with a bit of inspiration mixed with some good medical advice. Who knows if anyone will even read it? Yet, knowing how I feel right now—determined, yet scared—if I can make something that touches only one person in a positive way, then I will be happy enough. Hell, if it sits on my computer forever, I will still be glad I wrote it.

I'm writing it for myself. I'm writing it to remember what I'm feeling right now. I'm writing it to record what this journey asks of me. I'm writing it to coach myself through this, to keep my wits about me, to find the funny at the bottom of the chemo bag.

3

WINNING!

I am a board-certified chiropractic internist and nutritionist. I have twenty-one letters after my name, letters I worked hard for. If I work hard enough, I'll need both sides of the business card for all the letters I'm going to have. For now, I put my name on both sides of my cards. This way, no matter which side is up—say, when you try to throw it away but it falls onto the ground by the trash can—you see my name and know I'm always available.

For your healthcare needs, that is. That's an important distinction. And at a mutually convenient time, preferably in my office. Did that need to be said?

We want people to remember our names; our names stand in for everything we think about ourselves. But I think we are actually remembered for our stories. I don't want anyone to remember my name and nothing else. What is most important is the story of my journey. That's what will have the power to change a friend or a family member or even a stranger when someone tells it. I don't need the accolades (the letters after my name suffice); I want to affect people in a positive way on their own journeys.

I have been told before to write a book. The one I am writing right now is not what they meant, but we don't always get to choose these things.

When I counsel my patients, I really spend time with them. They tell me this is rare and unexpected for a medical encounter, which is unexpected for me because it's always been important to me to, you know, actually care for the people who come to me for help. Anyway, sometimes we'll discuss food and water choices and seeking out things that are organic, grass-fed, hormone-free, etc., and I'll say something like, "If I teach you to be perfect, you will be dead."

This is also unexpected, but that's the point.

That is, if you tried to avoid everything that was bad for you, you'd never eat or drink or do anything. Silly, I know, but I believe it. I believe it because our water and our food are so adulterated that, even if we buy or grow the best out there, we are still dealing with nutrient-deficient soil, contamination, deceit from manufactures, etc., etc. We can do the best we can and hope that it doesn't affect our environment—that is, our bodies—in a negative way over time.

I did all the right things because I know all the right things, and I still got sick. Think about that. It sucks. Talk about hindsight. I have been living my life, every waking minute making choices that, in that moment, I believed to be the best, most correct, most beneficial choice for my life—for my body or my mind or my family. Sometimes, moments later, the information changes and, in hindsight, you wish you had chosen differently. Sometimes it takes years before we get the right perspective. So, looking back, do I think I did all the right things? Sure, I did! I made educated choices. I made fun choices. I made choices that were not popular. I made choices that were mine to make.

Why, then, did I get sick? I have a bunch of ideas. I bet I will come up with a lot more before I'm through.

One of my rules is to avoid eating things that are not food. I won't eat M&M's because they have oxidized aluminum in them. I also hate chocolate, but even if I liked chocolate, I wouldn't eat M&M's. Did you know about the aluminum? Every bag of M&M's lists "Lake" among the ingredients. Right at the end. It says, "Blue 1 Lake, . . . Red 40 Lake, Blue 2 Lake, Yellow 6 Lake, Yellow 5 Lake." This is an example of how manufacturers deceive you with subtle sleight of hand. You think it's just food coloring—harmless, right? But lake contains oxidized aluminum. It is a toxic metal that can contribute to Alzheimer's disease, Parkinson's, and dementia[1]. I do a lot of genetic testing in my office, so of course I've done mine too. Alzheimer's is in my family history, and it turns out I have the activated ApoE ε4 gene, meaning I'm at risk. Thus, I won't touch M&M's.

I have gone dairy-free for twenty years, with the occasional cheat—who hasn't eaten the entire half gallon of strawberry ice cream in a depressive binge? I pay for that for forty-eight hours, and then I am good for another six months. About a decade ago, I went completely gluten-free because of annular granulomas on my hands. This is an autoimmune disease, and when you have it, you go gluten-free. You take vitamin D3, and you consume glutathione and the precursors to make it in the body. Incidentally, I've also noticed over the years that going gluten-free makes an enormous difference for patients with Hashimoto's thyroiditis, rheumatoid arthritis, psoriasis, and many other conditions. There are a number of theories about why this might be, my favorite being that gluten isn't what it used to be because of our industrial food system. It's a go-to nutrition

---

1   https://www.iospress.nl/ios_news/human-exposure-to-aluminum-linked-to-famil-ial-alzheimers-disease/

strategy for me for a lot of chronic and tricky conditions, and I recommend giving it a shot if you've got one of those.

But, as I was saying, I eat pretty damn healthy from a Western-diet perspective.

Okay, I do consume one whole bag of candy corn at Halloween. It always makes me sick to my stomach. It is ironic that I will choose something that makes me feel temporarily ill, and yet there are probably aspects of the healthy foods I choose regularly that have also contributed along the way.

Right after my CT scan, I knew I wasn't going be able to stop thinking about why I was sick.

December 23, 2013

> *I will have to share my theory about doctors getting sick. That's for another day. Right now, I don't feel like focusing any more on the word* sick.
>
> *I mean, right now, I feel great! I look well. Today, I answered the question, "How are you today?" with "I am well," and I meant it. That is not going to change. Because I'm going to stay well.*

When I began the process of trying to divorce my husband (and it is a process), he bought a Groupon for a trip to Costa Rica. Divorce isn't a switch—that's one thing I learned. You think you're announcing a decision, but it is received as a threat, as a warning that he's got to do something to save the ship from sinking. I kept saying, "No, you don't understand; we're already at the bottom of the sea," but he kept trying to plug the holes and find a lifeboat. If he had shown some of the same energy during the last thirteen years, we probably wouldn't have been getting divorced, but that was his lesson to learn, not mine.

No, divorce is a process. You think you've drawn a line that clearly marks the end of things, but really, you've just started having painful conversations and arguments in which you detail all the hurtful neglect over all the years. You think you'll be broken up, but he'll still be there in the house because he can't afford to get his own place. It's a muddled, confusing process of slowly disentangling yourself from the rigging of a wrecked ship, and that's how you find yourself going to Costa Rica for an adventure getaway with the man you don't want to even look at.

The Costa Rica tickets pissed me off, if I'm being honest. I had always wanted to travel, but he never wanted to go anywhere. Then he waits until I'm ready to leave to finally do something spontaneous and exciting? And he spends a bunch of our money to do it?

He suggested he could go alone or with a friend, but I said, "No way. I paid for those tickets, so I'm going." What I should have said was, "No way, those are my tickets now. I'm taking my friend Kristin." But again, that's not how divorce goes.

What I wanted to tell you about was the zip line course. In addition to the airfare, we got tickets for horseback riding and a zip line through the jungle. A zip line is basically just a rope between two poles that you traverse by hooking your harness up to a little wheelie thingy. For some reason, the starting platform, only large enough for several people to stand on, is a mesh grate that you can look through to remind yourself how easily you would die if you fell off this tiny ledge with no railings.

As the joke goes, it's not the falling I'm afraid of; it's the landing. And I'm honestly not even that afraid of going splat on the jungle floor. It would be scary for a few seconds, and then it would be over. What I'm really afraid of is falling and being incapacitated and lying there on the jungle floor until wild animals come and rip the meat off my bones. Maybe that's your thing, but it's not mine.

Here's the thing about that zip line course: there's no exit. Once you get up there and start, there's no way down until the end. My soon-to-be ex would have been able to only watch while the wolves and whatever they have in Costa Rica started picking at me. Or he could have zipped to the end and come back for me, but that would be asking a lot of that guy.

Getting a cancer diagnosis is like being scared of heights and being told you have to do eleven zip lines.

I told Lori, my workout buddy, about my diagnosis the day after I found out, and she went into action mode. "I'm so sorry," she said, "but I'm here for you. I'm going to be with you through this." I already knew that, though. That's Lori! She's a warrior. She texted me at 5:00 a.m. the next morning to ask how I was doing. She knew I'd be up and getting ready to exercise. I texted her back: "Winning."

That's my secret code word. I wish I could take credit for it, but it was her idea. We adopted it as our cancer theme. (She also promised me a girls' trip after our win, but no, I won't be telling about that. Ha! We are all talk and no bite anyway.)

So, there's a pickle, a cucumber, and a penis . . . but I am not telling the rest of the joke. You will have to read through a bunch more of my thoughts, feelings, and advice to find it. Curious, though, aren't you? It is a really good joke.

I guess I don't want to write a book just for myself. I want you to read it to the end. Put down your phone—no cheating—and keep reading!

4

PAY ATTENTION

Life is kind of wonderful—when you pay attention. When we don't, it slides by so fast. For me, it's about noticing little things that can mean so much. We tend to get caught up in wanting the big things, but those are few and far between compared to the little things, and at the end of the day I really believe the little things are more important.

December 24, 2013

Today was a fabulous day. Up at 3:30 a.m. Training with Bob at Athletic Republic. We did arms (twenty-eights) and core. Twenty-eights are when you do seven reps of an exercise in four different ways in quick succession, really taxing your muscles by changing how you make them work. These last two workouts have been so great because I am pissed, and I am going to push those time capsules to their max!

Maybe I should explain about the time capsules. It's one of those images that came to me that helped focus my energy. It was just that morning, in fact, during training. I was thinking about these lesions in my body—that's how they show up on a CT scan—and how, in a sense, they were an encapsulation of every choice I had made up to this point. Everything I'd eaten or drunk or breathed or put on my skin, every minute I spent exercising or lounging or working or playing. All my experiences, good and bad, led me to this point with these *things* inside my body.

And I'm not one to feel a lot of regret about my choices. I do what I do and accept the consequences, and as long as I felt it was right at the time, I generally feel pretty good about things. But these lesions, these alien bodies that somehow my own body created . . . these I could not accept. I just wanted them out. I couldn't change anything about how they got there—and maybe I couldn't have done anything different—but they irritated me; they didn't belong.

There I was on the floor doing abdominal work, and Bob was screaming at me to push harder and keep going, and I had this visual of the lesions inside me: I was pushing them out of my body and burying them. They were like tiny time capsules, these records of a moment in time, only they were the kind I wanted to bury and leave buried forever.

That was where I was. *I have these time capsules in my body, these little things trying to do me in, but I'm going to make them work for it. In fact, I'm going to exhaust them until they have no more fight in them or I have no more fight in me.*

I'm tenacious in a fight.

I spent the afternoon in my art studio throwing clay and getting messy and forgetting the world around me. There was no room for illness in my art! That was kind of ironic because being around clay had not been a healthy choice. I had used lead-based glazes and breathed in tons of dust from sanding my pieces. A few years before my diagnosis, I stopped sanding and changed to unleaded glazes, which made my pieces less stunning, but I knew it was better for me. Put pottery on my list of things I really didn't do perfectly. Probably should reconsider my desire to learn how to weld while I'm at it. I did take one welding class. Made a cute little tractor. I might have to take up photography. You don't need to work with chemicals anymore.

That night, I did something I had not really let myself do in too long. Steve, my soon-to-be ex, took the kids to his parents' for Christmas Eve, so no one was home. I had the house all to myself. I'm usually pretty boring on these occasions and more or less stick to my usual routine (I'm a Jewish girl; Christmas was always Steve's thing). That night, though, while I was cleaning the kitchen, I cranked the tunes and danced all around, getting lost in the music and the movement. Dancing makes me feel powerful and provides me a sense of freedom. I used to want to be a professional dancer, in fact. Maybe I'll tell that story sometime. If you haven't ever let loose when no one is watching, you are missing out. Your body was made to move. Try it. Go ahead. Like, right now. Put this down and just dance.

Come on. . . . *Now!*

When I had danced out what needed dancing out, I got an urge to clean my junk drawer in the kitchen. Everyone has one, right? Well, I have two, one in my bedroom and one in the kitchen; I never settle for being like everyone else.

Anyway, I came across three written pages that weren't dated, but I could tell they were written before my third child, Jackson, was born. Yes, I had cleaned the drawer in the last seven years, but I guess I never really looked at these three sheets.

They were a list of goals that I had written out—life goals for years to come, from stupid stuff to more interesting stuff. I sat down and looked them over to see how I was doing.

Own a boat. . . . Check.

Be interviewed on TV. . . . Does radio count? I've done that a couple times. Check.

Have fresh flowers delivered to my home once a week. . . . Check— Thanks, David. (David is my florist friend, and he's amazing. Tell him I sent you.)

Have a restaurant named after me. . . . What was I thinking when I wrote that one? At any rate, I'm still waiting. But my friend Larry wrote, produced, and played all the instruments in a song he wrote just for me. That feels at least as good as a restaurant, if not better.

Be known as an expert in my community. . . . Check.

Grow healthy children both emotionally and physically. . . . Let's call that one a work in progress, though I think they're doing pretty well.

Read two books a month. . . . Sometimes.

Leave in trust $1,000,000 for each child. . . . Working on that.

Have a net worth of $20 million. . . . I am also working on that.

Number sixty-six: Stay cancer-free. . . . Shit.

Okay, no reason to panic. Our goals change as the circumstances change. What did goal number sixty-six really mean except do what I could to prevent cancer if at all possible? I think I've done better than the average person and nearly as well as I know I can do.

But there I was, with cancer. Time to rewrite my goals. I had already started for 2014. I had eight days left to finish. Now I would include *Winning!* That was at the top, the bottom, and all over my

list. Lori and I even made headbands with *Winning!* printed on
them. Winning in life, in parenting, in medicine, in teaching, in
friendship, and in love. Oh, and occasionally at pai gow poker. I had
just learned how to play that a few weeks earlier at the casino in
Phoenix with my cousin Irwin. It is ridiculously easy if you know how
to play poker, and I have known since I was a kid. There were some
interesting people at my kitchen table when I was growing up, like
true-to-life mobsters. There was always a lot of money on our table,
and I would fill drinks, make popcorn, watch, and listen, and that is
how I learned. But I don't remember names or dates, so please don't
send the FBI after me. And, Your Honor, "I don't recall" will be my
standard answer. Some of that stuff I have to take to the grave.

But not yet. There is no other choice for me than to win.

December 24, 2013

I set an appointment for six days from now with a
lymphoma specialist: Dr. Bishop at the University
of Chicago. I wait and I focus on everything else
because between now and then, I will have no new
information.

I am cleaning up even more how I eat. I have
been dairy-free, gluten-free, and sugar-free for
years, but you know how that goes. You make little
exceptions here and there. From here on out, though,
everything will be super clean: no dairy, gluten,
sugar, or artificial colors or flavorings. Everything
fresh and raw, organic and grass fed. My treat is
hummus and rice cakes. I know some people would
rather eat cardboard, but I actually like both.
Drinking only reverse osmosis water (I put that in

years ago, and let me tell you, it is the only way to go) and lots of herbal tea.

Started a regimen of over one hundred pills a day. That takes up one meal and sixty ounces of water to get them all down. Then I would rinse and repeat the same routine two more times in a day. If you're wondering how someone could rack up a list of one hundred pills, well, here's a little taste:

alpha-lipoic acid	vitamin B complex	beta-glucans	colostrum
curcumin	essential fatty acids	garlic	glutathione
NAC	resveratrol	selenium	vitamins B12, C, D, E
turkey tail mushrooms	a ton of pancreatic enzymes		

So, yeah, a lot. I'm giving my throat muscles a workout like they've never known.

That day, I actually considered changing my profession. Only for a minute, but I still think being a physician contributed to my illness. I'm not going to leave my practice. I love what I do, and I am good at it. It might not be good for me, though. We can explore that later.

As soon as they knew about my diagnosis, everyone on my team reached out to me in different ways. I chose well. I always believed and was taught the best offense is defense. Defense wins games! I have seen that over and over in my kids' sports. *I am building the best defense ever,* I told myself.

Hmm . . . What if we had team jerseys with time capsules on them? That sounds so silly, but I thought I might have them made anyway. It's not every day you get cancer; might as well live it up a bit.

5

BOYS DON'T LIKE SHOPPING FOR PANTIES

I took my kids to Victoria's Secret after the holidays. There's nothing like taking your nine-year-old son into a store bedecked floor to ceiling with lacy bras and skimpy panties to take your mind off the malignant growth in your neck.

As soon as Ari (the aforementioned nine-year-old) realized where we were going, he got this uncomfortable look on his face, like a dog going to the veterinarian. Once inside, he became very still and stoic. He walked around, trying not to knock into any tables or even brush against the racks, as though they were covered in barbed wire. It was his own personal *Mission: Impossible.*

I tried so hard not to laugh because I'm a good mom, and it's not kind to laugh at your kids. He looked like he was being traumatized for life. I pictured him as an adult telling his therapist about his early initiation into the mysteries of the boudoir—with his mom, no less!— and describing this day when he had to stand next to a manikin (spelling intentional!) in a red vinyl corset.

The way I see it, if this really is important enough to come up in therapy, then we made a memory. I hope to create millions of memories (and keep the therapists in business) with my kids. The kids will appreciate that too, right?

This is what a great day looks like. Let's recap. *I am alive. I am out and about in the world. I am embarrassing my children like a normal parent.*

Even better, I felt fantastic. Really. I trained hard that day. Bob, my trainer and friend, kicked my ass with crazy push-ups, box jumps, way too much abdominal work, and whatever he felt he could torture me with. It was worth every drop of sweat.

Lori insisted I needed to let people into this thing with me, so I took her advice and assembled a team of friends whom I knew I could call when things got serious. I don't usually ask for help, but Lori had been through this with her brother who had a terrible experience and passed away. I trusted her, and, when it came down to it, I was scared enough that I could see the value of having a few people close to me through this. I asked my friend Kristin to be the third part of my team, to be there to help me when and if needed. Kristin is strong and positive and funny and supportive and loving (this is why I realized I should have gone to Costa Rica with her instead of my soon-to-be-ex-husband), and I knew she would be an asset in the future because she already had been since we became friends years ago.

My daughter, Reese, who was eleven, had sex ed that year, but she wasn't really interested in sexy stuff yet, except as a morbid curiosity. I saw her trying not to stare at the manikins (intended spelling—again!) in red and white teddies in the store windows.

"What do you think?" I asked her.

She scowled, seemingly confused. "What are these even for?"

It was a very practical question about a very impractical garment. "Women wear them to turn on their boyfriends," I said.

She thought about this for a second and seemed to realize, with an expression of shock not unlike her brother's, what this meant. "Do they . . . do it . . . with them on?" she asked in apparent disbelief.

"Sometimes," I said.

She scowled again. "And then they wear them again? How gross."

"They can be washed, you know."

Reese walked away with her own mild trauma, thinking about the weird things humans do in private. I walked away, thinking we'd need a lesson, tomorrow, on how to work the laundry machines.

Jackson, my youngest, sprayed himself with all the feminine scents until he smelled like a spilled fruit salad in a flower shop.

"Can I get this one?" he asked, holding up something that looked pink and expensive. I told him no. He asked about another one. I told him I wasn't going to buy him women's perfume, and then it was his turn to get emotional. He was barely seven; I could live with myself for upsetting him over that. Besides the idea of him walking around smelling like "Bombshell" or "Temptation" or whatever it was, I didn't need him spraying all those chemicals all over the house.

I made my purchases—which were neither teddies nor perfume—and we left. That was it. No big lessons, no brilliant insights, just a mom and her kids going to the store. But every day I get to spend making traumatic memories with my kids is a gift. Every night I get to kiss my kids good night is a gift. Some nights as I was going through chemo, they tucked me in since they usually stayed up later than me when the treatments I chose made me tired. Do they understand how important it is that we are together?

That night, I wrote in my journal:

> *What will tomorrow bring? It doesn't matter, in one sense, because I will see the beauty in it and share that with those I love. My amazing, fantastic, wonderful journey is truly underway, and it will be nothing short of exactly what I choose to make it.*

A year before, would I have thought anything about such an episode? I might have laughed about it with my girlfriends, but then I'd probably have forgotten about it. What, after all, does it really mean, in the grand scheme of things? But I journaled about this with the intention that it might be seen one day by others—and here you are, reading it. So I can take the time to say it felt significant and nice to do something so normal and wonderful with my kids.

That was Spencer's idea. The book, that is. At one point, he even offered to be my coauthor. He wrote a book himself, and when he gifted me a copy, he wrote in it, *The next one we do together.* I assumed the subject matter would be much different than this—you know, something in our field of expertise—but here we are.

6

CINDY'S FOOD AND POOP RULES

(MY CLEANEST CHAPTER!)

When Reese was nine, she came home one day from school and said, "Mom, I want a Lunchables for my lunch."

To say I freaked out would be an understatement. You'd think she'd told me she was pregnant with triplets and the father was fifty-two years old and they were getting married. My blood pressure jumped up, and I'm guessing my eyebrows became red flames.

"What? You listen to me: You will never, *never*, eat a Lunchables. I will never *buy* a Lunchables; you will never *consume* a Lunchables. And you can go back and tell your friends whose mothers are buying them Lunchables that their parents are *poisoning* them!"

At some point, I had gotten up in her face with my finger pointing at her, something I never do with my kids. What had come over me? Rest assured, she never asked for a Lunchables again. I'm surprised she ever asked for anything ever again . . . except maybe makeup. That was only going to be a matter of time.

Everybody knows I keep a clean pantry, meaning we eat very clean. I'm dairy-free and gluten-free. While I was walking through cancer, I went 100 percent sugar-free too. Keep all that carcinogenic, inflammatory shit away from me. "I'm not totally crazy about it," I would tell people. "I eat dairy-free ice cream once in a while." I'd have red meat or a glass of wine. But then and now, when I go to the store, you won't see Twinkies or pop or mac-and-cheese mix in my cart. There are lots of fruits and veggies, lots of fresh foods. Ingredients that sound like things that grow rather than things that were created in a lab are the better choice.

Food is so important to our health. If I learned anything in school, it was that. We treat food like it's about getting rid of that hungry feeling or about enjoyment, and of course it is, but more than that, it's about providing our bodies with the fats, proteins, carbohydrates, nutrients, and calories we need to keep our cells, tissues, bones, and organs functioning properly. Our bodies are pretty efficient and skilled at repairing themselves and filtering out bad stuff, but you have to give them enough of the good stuff, or they start running into problems.

I estimate 80 percent of my clients wouldn't need me if they simply ate well. Reducing inflammation by cutting out sugar, dairy, and gluten can do wonders. Fresh, clean food helps with clear blood vessels, happy synapses, and an efficient and clean digestive tract. Many people don't realize they have a gluten sensitivity or are eating a high-inflammation diet, and if they only experimented with an elimination diet, they might discover cutting out one thing could solve a lot of problems.

All that stuff we get that's in boxes or bags or handed through a drive-through window—I don't even call it food. It's chemicals. If you can leave it for a couple days and it still looks like itself instead of brown or green and gross, it's probably not food. Like, literally. If it doesn't go bad, that means the microorganisms that make real food spoil or go bad cannot find any nutrition in that thing.

Food is something you can fish for, slaughter, or pick off a vine or tree. It is something that grows or eats and still belongs to the food chain. It's seeds, nuts, beans, fresh veggies and fruit, fresh fish, organic and grass-fed meat. It doesn't need anything added to make it do something it wasn't meant to do like sit in your fridge for a month. As soon as you start adding things, when you chemically alter or otherwise adulterate them, you've created a manufactured product. In addition, the hormones, antibiotics, and pesticides we use to grow our food find their way into our bodies and are having a cumulative effect we're still unraveling.

Again, we're not perfect in my house. We're pretty good, but we're not perfect. Certainly, once I got my diagnosis, I got much stricter. I cut out sugar in addition to gluten and dairy, and I was very careful to order from the gluten-free menu if I ever went out. Most of the time, I preferred not to go out but to make everything at home. I do love red meat, but I cut back on that and ate more fish and chicken. I'm not a big candy person anyway, but during treatment, you could have put a big bag of candy on my desk and walked away, and it would have all been there whenever you came back. I simply removed it as an option for myself.

And really, I don't care if you want to eat chemicals. Go to McDonald's if that's what you want to do. Buy the prepackaged, manufactured food. I get it; it's easy, convenient; life can be busy. No judgment, really. But understand what you're eating isn't food. It's a choice, but there's nothing healthy or nutritious about it. Don't lie to yourself about what you're choosing to put into your body, right?

Education is the key ingredient for me. You come in to see me with back pain; I'm going to ask you about food. And poop. And I'm going to educate you a bit if you need it because eating well will help your back problem heal.

The same goes with my kids. I can't control what they eat anymore, but I tried to educate them. I used to pack a protein and a fruit or vegetable for their lunches. Maybe a salad, maybe plain carrots. No ranch dressing in this house. Of course, they would get made fun of for their lunches. Kids learn quickly that our society values junk food and that people who try to eat healthy are "weird." My kids would come home and report that their food was "boring." So there was trading. My kids would tell me they traded for a Snickers bar because I didn't let them have that. I could never figure out how anything I had packed for them was worth a Snickers bar to some other kid, unless the rest of that kid's diet was so unhealthy, something in his cells was saying, "Yes, please, get the carrots!"

The Lunchables thing maybe indicates that I'm at least a little crazy about food choices. That was before the cancer too. But I know too much about what that stuff can do to us. I stand in line at the checkout counter and, truth be told, I'm mortified. I think, *Oh my G-d, there's diabetes on the belt in front of me and cancer in the cart behind me and obesity behind that and over there and over there . . .* Jackson comes home with bags of chips, and I say, "You know, that—" and he interrupts me and says, "Will give me cancer. Yeah, I know."

Recently, I called my son "Walking Diabetes." Type 2 that is, as in if you make poor food choices, this is the one you may get. Type 1 is a whole different animal. Maybe when he's on his own, he'll hear my voice in his head when he's at the store, and if it stops him from buying one bag of candy, it's worth it to me. These effects are additive, after all. Ari will say, "Come on; will one or two candy bars cause cancer?" And, of course, he's right. If you eat one bag of M&M's, you probably will not be severely sick; however if it becomes a staple in your diet for years, you may find yourself with a challenge you didn't see advertised in the commercials.

Growing up, I did not learn a healthy relationship with food. My parents both ate very unhealthy diets with lots of salty, fatty snacks and sweets. If my sister and I tried to help ourselves to something, though, my mother would say, "You don't need that."

I used to think, *But it's in the house. Doesn't that mean we can eat it?* No, it meant my dad could eat it. We kids "didn't need it." The message: *Food is about control.* Dad got to make the decisions; children didn't.

Meanwhile, my dad would eat an entire Sara Lee pound cake and drink a can of chocolate syrup for dessert. I still can't believe it. There's another bad message: *When you do get to choose what you eat, you can eat a lot of whatever junk you want!* Lucky me, I don't really care for chocolate, or I might have picked up that habit. Pound cake, though, is another story.

Of course, we also had the familiar rule about cleaning our plates before we left the table. "There are starving children in Europe," my mom would say, to which we'd respond, "Then pack this up and send it to them." That never worked, and instead, we had to clear our plates. The message: *Eat whether you're hungry or not*, which led to a lifetime of overeating.

I'm over fifty now, and I still struggle with this stuff. When I'm eating out and feel full, I need the server to take my dish away immediately, or I will keep picking at it just for something to do and because a little voice in the back of my head is saying it's wasteful to leave it there. With my kids, however, I fight to change things. I have never, ever made them clear their plates. They know that if they're full, they can stop eating, and we can always pack up their food for later. I don't mention the starving people anywhere else in the world because it isn't practical to send them our food; I don't want to get into a conversation about whether we should be shipping their dinner overseas.

When my kids were little, they got what I ate, via my breast milk, by far my greatest contribution to their diet. After they sprouted teeth, we were off to try some mushed-up bananas and other fruits. I knew there was an expected order, but I jumped into avocados and mangos early. I ate them; so should my kids. No one even knew what a French fry was, let alone a fast-food French fry, until their dad took them through a drive-through many years later. In my house, we were dairy-, candy-, and fast-food-free for as long as I had a say—and as long as they had no friends and no car keys.

My control of my kids' lunchboxes was about setting healthy patterns before their prefrontal cortexes had fully developed. It worked for a while.

We might have swung too far in the other direction, though. Jackson had a friend, Isaiah, who lived down the street. Isaiah's parents worked, but his grandma Judy watched the kids after school, and Jackson loved hanging out with Isaiah at his house. I finally had to say, "You know; you can have Isaiah over here sometimes." He said, "Yeah, but Grandma Judy lets us go in the candy drawer whenever we want." I had created a kid who could not pass up the opportunity to have the forbidden food.

So, now I have Cindy's Food Rules. These are things I tell my patients, the simple things (I think) that can make shopping a little easier and eating a whole lot healthier:

1. Eat things that can be grown in the ground, picked off a tree or vine, slaughtered, or fished for.
2. If you can't pronounce the ingredients, it's not real food.
3. One nonfood item a week probably won't kill you. Several nonfood items a day might.
4. Drink lots of water. More than you think. (Although there is zero research to support drinking at least half your body weight in ounces of water a day, that is what "they" taught us. Who is "they"? Better to check your labs for dehydration; check your urine to make sure it is light in color and not a golden yellow. Heck, I am a physician. I still can't help giving advice once in a while.)

I'm not trying to scare anyone. Unless that would be motivating. You can't make good decisions if you don't know what counts as a good or bad decision. You can't stay healthy if you don't understand what's unhealthy about your food choices.

The other side of eating is pooping. In Chinese medicine, they believe immune health begins in the gut. If the gut isn't healthy, you're not healthy. Health problems in one area of your body might be related to problems in another.

They live this out in China still. I traveled there around 2000, and I was fascinated by how the public toilets worked. In the first place, you're crouching over a trough or hole rather than sitting. Not only that, but the attendant gives you only one square of single-ply toilet paper to take in there with you. Most Americans freak out when they hear that story, but the truth is, if you're eating real food, you won't really need toilet paper. Your poop will come out clean. The paper is only there to confirm you didn't need it.

You can tell I'm a lot of fun at parties. You should come to one of my seminars!

Sometimes I'll tell the China story and have a patient who says, "Oh yeah, it's great when that happens." I say, "That shouldn't be a once-in-a-while fun surprise. That should be every day."

If you come see me about that back pain, be prepared to have some real talk about poop. Not that I'm your mom and need to know everything, but if you want me to help you get healthy, we need to treat your body as an interconnected organic system rather than a machine with interchangeable parts.

How often do you go? Is it runny or solid? Wide or skinny? How long is it, or is it like little rabbit pellets? Does it smell bad? Do you see undigested food in there (other than corn)? We go through a whole routine of questions, and from there I can tie what you're eating to allergies, asthma, immune disease, signs of cancer—even mental health stuff.

Early in my career, I saw a child who had been kicked out of two schools because of his impulsive and problematic behavior. His mom was desperate for this third school to work, and she didn't want to medicate him. After talking to them and doing some hands-on work, I recommended a stool function study. We found parasites. *Parasites!* He had none of the normal physical symptoms, but I suspected the behavioral stuff was related. Sure enough, we cleaned up his gut, and the behaviors disappeared within weeks. As far as we knew, the school assumed he'd been medicated, but the important thing was they didn't kick him out.

Some of you parents are starting to get interested now. I'm going to have poop kits on display next to this book when I go on tour.

"Poop kits! Get your poop kits here! Funny cancer book and poop kit bundle on sale now!" Really, though, if I give you a poop kit, I can analyze what your body is excreting and tell you things about yourself that would shock you.

My colleagues laugh at me because no matter what I'm speaking on, we always end up taking a couple minutes to talk about poop. Often longer. But there's a reason for that: people don't understand that it's important. If I have a captive audience, that's my opportunity.

Like, lots of people don't even look at it. They can't even gauge their health because they're not collecting the information they need. Do you know, for instance, that your poop should be soft to firm in texture and sausage shaped? Or that you should poop once or twice a day? I had a patient once who hadn't pooped in thirty-one days! You don't need a degree to know something's wrong there.

Here's a conversation I've had more than a few times.

"I'm going to ask you about poop. How are your bowel movements?" I ask.

"Oh, they're fine. Normal," they respond.

"What's normal? How often?"

"Maybe every three days?"

"Do you only eat every three days?"

"No, I eat three times a day."

"Well then, you're marinating in waste material, because you need to be pooping."

I know this makes some people uncomfortable. We were taught not to talk about these things, but I don't know how you're supposed to learn something is healthy or unhealthy if we don't have that conversation.

So, while I have your attention, here's my quick primer on pooping:

1. You should be pooping once or twice a day. Some people will say you should go at least three times per day, but if you're eating actual food, one to three times a day is normal. If you poop once a week, that is common, not normal.
2. Your poop should be medium to dark brown, soft to firm in texture, and pretty consistent day to day. If it's a strange color and you didn't have hot sauce or green beer or something the night before, something may be up.
3. It shouldn't smell like roses, but it shouldn't smell really bad. I should be able to walk past the bathroom and not know you pooped.
4. It should be sausage shaped. You know, like your intestines. Some say like a banana. I say just not like little rabbit pellets.
5. It should not hurt to pass. If it's regularly painful or difficult, you should look at your diet and talk to your healthcare provider. (I'm online if you want to come find me!)

Okay, that wasn't too uncomfortable, was it? (If it was, you should talk to your doctor!) This is important stuff. There are maybe two or three takeaways I want readers to get from this book, and one is that understanding food and poop is key to being healthy.

The others are that we have choices in how we approach our lives, and that you shouldn't live with anyone; you should buy a duplex.

Maybe, also, think about your attitudes about food so you don't turn into a psychotic demon when your child wants a Lunchables.

7

"BOOBY" CAN BE A BIG WORD

Two days into 2014, I wrote the year right. We always get excited when the year changes and laugh about how we can never remember to write it correctly. Humans are silly that way, but that day, I was in the mood to find it charming. It's one of those little things, and that day I was paying attention to the little things, like words and how people react to them.

Why? Because each little thing contributes to the big things; they're like the backdrop to the big things, helping the big things stand out. And there is such beauty in little things. Sometimes they can become big things just because someone pays attention to them.

I drove to my office on that first workday of the new year. When I looked in my rearview mirror, there was the most beautiful rainbow behind me. Had I not taken the time to look behind me, I would not have seen it. It lifted my spirit in such a way that I almost ran off the road trying to take a picture of it while driving fifty-five miles per hour.

I said I was paying attention to little things; I never said I would stop doing stupid things.

We were in the middle of a polar vortex in Chicago, which meant the Great Plains had become a frozen tundra. On New Year's Day, it was −17°F with a windchill of −46. On January 2, it started at −12. Everyone was told to stay home; school was canceled for a second day; and the snowdrifts were huge.

While everyone was freaking out about the dangerous cold and only half joking about the end of the world, here is what I saw: I got where I wanted to go with less traffic—what a bonus! I'd had a little extra winter break with my kids. We'd had a blast skidding around the street in the drifts like it was an amusement park ride.

I read so many complaints on Facebook about the weather, but I thought it was an amazing opportunity to discover things. Some people actually have it bad, but my Facebook friends don't. What's the point of being miserable then? The snow on the trees is beautiful. A lot of people in the world never get to experience that gift. Think about that. It's kind of a shame. If you have never seen snow, go see it. Snow is magical. After you dance in your kitchen, go find a tundra, put on some Moon Boots (anyone remember those?), and go play in some fluffy, crunchy snow. You won't be sorry, just cold.

I hadn't written in over a week. I thought about doing it quite a few times. Sometimes thoughts are too private to write, and sometimes there are no words. I spend a lot of time picking out the right words to say and taking back ones I don't like and asking people's forgiveness when I can't find the ones I want. I tell my kids that words can't hurt you unless you let them. Because it's true they can sometimes hurt you.

I believe that words can empower and lift other human beings to places they didn't realize they could go. But you have to at least attempt to be precise. Nothing is *always* true or *never* right, for example, yet we use these words so freely and incorrectly. I want to pick my words carefully, every day.

I like these words from the neuroscientist Dr. Joe Dispenza in *Breaking the Habit of Being Yourself*:

> *When you are living in survival, you are trying to control or force an outcome; that's what the ego does. When you're living in the elevated emotion of creation, you feel so lifted that you would never try to analyze how or when a chosen destiny will arrive. You trust that it will happen because you have already experienced it in mind and body—in thought and feeling. You know that it will because you feel connected to something greater. You are in a state of gratitude because you feel like it's already happened.*

For me, words create the emotion that will determine the outcome. For instance, in January 2014, I had cancer, but if I let that pull me into survival mode, I realized I'd literally go crazy. After all, I *hate* not being in control. It's like I tell my kids: Control the things you can control. Then worry quietly to yourself about the things you can't.

I leave out that last part.

Here are the words I spoke in order to create the outcome I wanted: *I am healthy! I see life. I see energy. I see a fit body. I see an educated mind. I see passion and the ability to love deeply. I see courage and strength, and I see laughter.*

✚

I made a point to thank people around me for being important and for being present. Sometimes being present is all it takes to be important. Being in hell with a friend has to be better than being in hell all by yourself. But I wasn't really even in hell. Not yet, anyway.

It is amazing how many people are uncomfortable with being thanked. I feel like we say thank you to people all the time for doing us a favor or buying us a drink, but when you thank someone for something truly important, it gets awkward.

But, look: I was a pretty straightforward person before; if anything, getting cancer only sharpened my edges. I value my friends, and I will constantly remind them of it, so they're going to have to get used to it.

I want to laugh every day. Like, it's almost an item on my to-do list:

- Exercise.
- Stop at the bank.
- Laugh at something.

Not long after my diagnosis, I laughed because Jackson picked up two donut holes—one plain, one chocolate—held them up to his chest, and said proudly, "I have one white booby and one brown booby."

I had to laugh. My ridiculous little boy. Did he know I needed a laugh right then? Did he know that a little word like *booby* could become a big word with the help of a couple donut holes?

Of course, my brain went to trying to figure out what exactly was going on in his brain. When he describes people's skin at all, he talks about his friends who are brown and his friends who are peach. I think that makes sense, as our skin really is more peach than white. One of Jackson's first friends when we moved to our current home was Black. Jackson had asked, "When will I be as tan as Dylan?" I laughed and with 100 percent confidence assured him that was an impossibility. But what was he thinking now? Was he being literal about the color of the donut holes, or was he thinking about the colors we call people? Why did he think a donut hole was like a booby, anyway? Why didn't he say he had a peach booby?

I wonder if when the kids learned about my diagnosis, they understood there are different cancers with potentially different outcomes. Breast cancer gets a lot of publicity. Everyone knows the pink ribbon. . . . Our local football team wore pink socks for a week to bring awareness to breast cancer, until the daughter of one of our board members got leukemia. Then they learned about the orange ribbon. She passed away young. Maybe kids only really learn when someone they know has a different type of cancer. I didn't hang up any ribbons. I just wanted the kids to keep going the way we always had: with a yard that had good landscaping, blooming flowers, and no ribbons.

8

THe CHARACTeRS iN YOuR CANCeR STORY

You used to believe you had played some role in choosing your friends, in whom you surrounded yourself with and made room for in your life. You'd left that horrible fiancé and chosen Steve, after all. You chose whom you friended on Facebook and whom you talked to at the gym or, more likely, whom you avoided.

Then you started to tell people you have cancer, and Cancer—big "C" cancer—took pruning shears to your relationships. People you thought were going to be there became awkward and distant. People you only sort of knew became essential. Cancer was a gardener, but it was also a magnifying glass, enlarging the details that you hadn't seen before or did not want to see.

You want to tell people: Cancer will take people out of your life, but it will also bring them into your life. You must allow all these things to happen, or you're going to drive yourself crazy.

You will stop going to your book club because your life will become busier and book club feels more like a lots-of-time-to-myself activity, but book club is where you used to hang out with Karen, who said she would be there for you. You'll learn, and you'll tell other people, that the best thing you can do about Karen when Cancer brings her onstage is to have a backup plan.

You won't want to fault Karen too much—you kind of always had her number. She's the type of person who picks up friends and drops them like TV shows or favorite restaurants. When she's into you, she's into you, but when she's done with you, she's done with you. You have a similar attitude toward those in your book group. They are fun to hang around with for book group, but you don't need them outside of that setting.

Except Karen will make a point of seeking you out, prying into your affairs, and vowing her friendship to you. Karen will find out about your divorce and, who knows, may even start a rumor or two, not because she's nasty but because she won't think about your feelings. Karen will say, "If there's anything I can do, just let me know. Anything, really." Lots of people say that, but Karen will insist she really means it. That she's not like other people.

There will come a time when Lori will have a conflict and won't be able to drive you to chemo. Lori, whom you met at the gym, and for some reason the two of you hit it off. When you go to the gym, you like to give folks a friendly wave, then put your earbuds in and get down to it. You never train with anyone else, but Lori will be different. Lori is a bodybuilder and shares your love of weight training. She got you excited about training harder; you became training friends. You will visit Lori for lunch at her house one day and tell her about Cancer, and Lori will say, "Don't worry. I'm going to help you through this."

And she will.

Lori will drive you to all the appointments because they'll make you get a ride home. Lori will prepare a lunch and bring it because she knows you're going to get hungry, and she will be right, and you will be so glad Lori is there because you hadn't thought about it and would have just sat there feeling hungry and careless.

Lori will be your warrior, and you hope everyone has a warrior. In fact, you believe that life will usually bring a warrior to you if you need one.

But Lori is just one person with her own life and family, and one day she won't be able to drive you, so you'll rack your brain for someone who is home during the day, and you'll think of Karen. You'll call Karen, and she'll drop everything and pick you up in a limo because that's what she said she'd do.

Except she doesn't. Instead, she says, "Isn't there someone else?" and then, "Yeah, okay, I guess I can do that." She will pick you up in a nice but regular car with a sour look on her face and will pout all the way to your appointment. While they hook you up and start the drip, she will be on her phone instead of keeping you company, and she'll keep stepping outside to smoke.

She will make it quite clear this is an imposition and she'd rather be clipping her nails in front of the TV with a glass of Riesling than fulfilling her vow to be there for you when you needed her. Every stupid expression and scoff and sigh that comes from her direction will punish you for calling her bluff on the being-a-halfway-decent-friend thing.

Then she will put the cherry on top and suddenly get up and leave. "I didn't know it was going to take this long," she'll say. "I have something to do; I can't give you a ride home." She will just leave you there at the hospital with life-saving drugs flowing into your veins and no way home.

And it will piss you off. You didn't really expect much better from her, you tell yourself, except you kind of did because she insisted that you could rely on her for exactly this kind of thing. You would rather she had lied to you (and you hate being lied to) and not gotten involved than to have said she'd help and then been bitchy the whole time. Half the reason you called her was to give her the chance to do the thing she said she would; it seemed important to her.

So, yeah, you will be pissed. And it will hurt, because it always hurts when you make yourself vulnerable to someone, even if it's just for a ride, and they choose to make you feel your dependence on them. As if *you* were the weak one, not them.

When Cancer brings Karen onstage, trust that gut instinct that says she wants all the accolades of a good performance without having to show up for rehearsal. That is why you will want a backup plan when it comes to dealing with Karen.

On the six-year anniversary of your last day of treatment, you get a text from Lori. It reads, "I always think about you around now. Congrats on six years! Love, Lori." It's strange, but you don't really talk to Lori anymore. You see her online and exchange the occasional text, but you don't see her all the time and tell her everything that's going on and laugh about the weird things happening to your body or cry about the pain and the fear. But she still thinks about you.

That's the role Lori will play. She will be loyal and fierce and will fight battles you didn't know needed fighting. She will sit with you during chemo and put up with all your obnoxious jokes, and she will feel like the most important person in your life, more than your husband (as if) or your kids, because she is the one person who doesn't need anything from you. She's the one person who lets you need things from her.

Lori will text you at any time of day just because she's thinking of you. She'll ask how you're doing, and you'll be honest, but truthfully, you're probably going to say, "Winning!" because that is still the code word, the word that means, "Every day is a battle, but I am out of bed and facing it."

When Cancer cues Lori to come onstage, you must learn to do two things. First, you must embrace her Lori-ness. You must allow her to do all the things she does to be your rock and your buttress and your chauffeur. She's there to take care of you when you can't or won't do it for yourself. You must trust that she is not Karen; she really wants to help you and will not hold it against you. You must love Lori for this and simply be a grateful recipient.

The second thing you must do is let her go. It will be sad, in its way, because you were so close during such a raw, hard time in your life. You will think, *How could a friendship forged in this much suffering ever end?* But you will not understand, yet, that people are always more complicated than they appear.

Lori's brother died of cancer before you even became friends. It was a terrible time for her, and her brother did not get the kind of compassionate and essential care he should have. Lori will be walking around with open wounds that you were too absorbed in your own life to see. You will feel a little bad about that, which is okay, but Lori didn't ask you to be careful about her wounds. Instead, she devoted herself to you because, you will see, years down the road, she needed to have a "good" cancer experience. She needed to walk with you and Cancer in a healthy, joyful, connected way so she could get some kind of closure for the loss of her brother.

That's why, years later when you and Lori meet again for coffee, you will be happy to see one another, and you will thank her over and over again and mean every word, but the conversation will feel stilted and bumpy. You will both feel gratitude for the meeting but contentment about the relationship having thinned out like it has.

Lori will play her role in your life, and you will play your role in her life, and when you have played your parts, that act will be over. There will be no reason to force things to go any further, but there will be eternal gratitude.

9

IF THE GUITAR CENTER SELLS GUITARS, WHAT'S THE CANCER CENTER SELLING?

When I call the Oncology department, they pick up and say, "The Cancer Center!" I don't like it. They should answer, "The Wellness Center!" After all, I am not calling to get cancer; I am calling to get well.

We know this in the chiropractic world and always name our businesses with words like *health*, *wellness*, and *alignment*. You know: the things we want you to have after you come see us.

My business is called Innovative Health and Wellness Center because I help teach you how to get and be well, and sometimes that requires innovative thinking and testing. Doesn't that make more sense?

When I was in treatment and they answered the phone with "The Cancer Center!" I thought I should respond, "Yes, I'd like some Hodgkin's and maybe a throat cancer while I'm at it. Do you have anything on special?" Hey, I had cancer; maybe cut me some slack for needing a shot of dark humor with my poisonous chemo cocktail once in a while.

If I were in charge of the world (and I should be, for at least a day), I would make it illegal to use any illness or disease in the name of a practice or center. How about "Thanks for calling the Beautiful, Successful, Joyful, Filled-with-Love-and-Laughter Healing Company of People Like You Who Are Fabulous"? Okay, a little awkward; I'm not a marketer. But you catch my drift. And if you don't, you're welcome to move off this planet because I am in charge now, and you are affecting my energy in a negative way. *Ugh!*

Having lunch with my friend Wendy, I told her, "I don't want to say, 'I'm sick.' I don't feel sick, I don't want to act sick, I don't want people treating me like I'm sick."

"Then say you're 'walking through cancer,'" she suggested.

Yes. *I am not sick. I am walking through cancer.* Sick happens to you; walking is something you do. If I were in charge of the world, I would give Wendy some important cabinet position or something so she could say wise things like that to me every day. So I decided from there on I no longer had cancer; I would be experiencing or walking through cancer.

So, I know I've been talking a big game about winning and being brave, but being brave doesn't mean not being scared, and I was terrified for Friday. Friday, I was meeting with Dr. Bishop for my biopsy results. How does one prepare for that appointment? What does one wear? Should I have someone with me? It's not like those gender reveal parties where they bake the results into a cake and everyone gathers around. "Surprise, it's malignant!"

I listed myself as my own primary care doctor at the hospital, so there was a chance I would see results before I spoke with my doctor. As in, a chance I would log in to the program and peek. Pretty scared of that too. It would be my CT scan all over again. Would it be better to know right away or to hear it from my doctor so I could fire a million questions at him and at least convince myself someone was in control of the situation?

The biopsy happened because I referred myself to the University of Chicago for it. The night before my surgery, I don't know if I looked nervous, but I got a big, worried hug from Reese. She asked a bunch of questions about what would happen to me during surgery, and I did my best to answer her honestly. In some ways, it helped to have my kid to deal with; it took some of my attention off myself.

At one point, she asked, "How exactly are they going to get the lymph node out?"

Jackson answered for me and told her, "They're going to take a chain saw to her neck and cut it out!" He says the funniest things, but at least he hadn't caught my nervousness. It would make a good YouTube video, though: a surgeon in a Carhartt jacket carving my lymph node out of my neck with a chain saw like one of those ice sculptors. Why aren't I in charge of the world again? Or maybe I missed my calling as a YouTube entertainer. Surely there's a market out there for people who want to laugh at cancer parodies. . . .

My amazing friend Lori promised to pick me up at 5:00 a.m. to go to U of C for the biopsy. I woke up at 3:00 a.m., surprised that I actually slept at all. I was ready. I called Spencer and was able to hear some inspiring words from him.

"You're strong and brave," he said. "I am so impressed by the way you're handling this battle in your life."

I listened closely and wanted to believe him, but it felt like that speech would be better saved for when my results came in. I am brave . . . most of the time, but I didn't feel like I'd done anything yet.

The hospital is this beautiful blue-and-red-and-glass building that juts out of the trees like an ocean liner cruising the South Side of Chicago. It's nice that insurance reimbursement for specialty services is still good. I left Lori in the waiting room and was walked by some nurses to pre-op. I was joined by a much older man, so I told the women walking us, "Hey, thanks for finding me a date."

The gentleman said to me, "You know, I have been married for forty-six years. Do you want to know the key to a happy marriage?"

"Sure," I responded, which strikes me now as weird, as I wanted out of my marriage so badly and right then, I was decidedly *not* interested in going down that path again. I did want to be passionately in love and share my life, but with a much different perspective this time around. My past mate choices were less than fantastic. I could write another book about this.

In other words, I was not looking for someone to save my marriage.

He was sweet, though, and told me, "On my tenth wedding anniversary, I took my wife to Europe. I am a really nice guy. On our forty-fifth anniversary, I went back to pick her up." *Ba-dum-bum.*

What a great way to ease the anxiety we were feeling about our procedures. You have to love charming older people and their silly jokes, the way they treat everyone like we're their grandkids. If our walk had been longer, I would have told him about my duplex theory. I still think that is one of my more brilliant ideas, and I'll cover that later in the book; don't worry. I am sad that I did not ask his name or what he was having done. I hope he is well and that he recovered to tell that joke a thousand more times.

Jocelyn welcomed me to pre-op. We joked about this and that. When I am nervous, I talk a lot. I mean, a lot more than I usually do. She was great, had been with the hospital for twenty-five years. I got naked, which I am actually okay with. I hung my clothes in a hanging clothes bag. Nice touch! The gown and socks were a pale lime green.

"Awesome," I told Jocelyn. "They're usually blue, and I hate blue."

"Lucky you," she said.

Green is a color of healing. Think growth and renewal, like the life cycle of plants. I wonder if someone considered that when they chose the color we would all wear before being sliced open. Patients pay enough for this hospital that I hope someone took the time to think through things like that.

I walked down the hall with my ass hanging out of my gown, and I have to tell you, I was okay with that too. I had worked hard on my ass and legs over the last year, and it looked great hanging out of the gown.

Then I peed in a cup. I guess I'm an overachiever, because you only need three drops and a few minutes to see if you are bringing a new life into this world, but I filled the cup.

"Congrats," Jocelyn said. "Not pregnant."

"I could have told you that!"

I remember the first time I found out I was pregnant. I was in the middle of one of my DABCI weekends (a chiro school post-doc thing—the acronym stands for Diplomate of the American Board of Chiropractic Internists) when the lab called me with the results. Cool that I could order my own test and order it *stat*. Reese was my Two-Martini Accident, but those martinis brought the most tenacious, strong, courageous, beautiful girl into my life.

Jocelyn told me my blood pressure was 122/78, which was high for me, though still considered normal. Remember, I was a little nervous. Next, the resident came in, and it was time to get stabbed with the IV.

"You've got one shot at this," I said, and I was only half joking. I hate needles; a bad experience in the hospital as a kid ruined me. I knew it was a fear I could overcome, but I didn't want to start on that particular day. Thankfully, I'm a lot better on the other side of the needle. I do blood draws all the time in my office, and I have yet to pass out on the patient. That would be awkward, wouldn't it?

As I gripped the bed, I knew the second the resident put the needle in that she had missed.

"Oh, sorry," she said.

"Yeah." I winced. "I still like you anyway," which may not have been entirely true.

How dumb is protocol? They tell you not to drink from midnight on, which dehydrates your veins and makes them collapse more easily. Guess what? No water: collapsed vein. Now try to get a needle in there. Really, I have vascular hands; I could do this on myself with my eyes closed. I told her to get someone who could do this, because I didn't want her to try it again.

The experienced anesthesiologist enters the story here. Kind of like clockwork with these folks, which is actually pretty interesting, how things just flow in hospitals. She had ten years on me, thank goodness. I am all for teaching and learning—after all, I was green as a physician at one point—but I am no longer in the mood to be a science experiment. As she told the twelve-year-old to do the IV, I said, "No. I already had one miss; I am *not* doing this another time." The anesthesiologist got me no problem, like I knew she would. She stood and spoke with confidence, conviction, and a fabulous bedside manner. None of that can be taught. You have it or you don't, and she had it. I told her so and thanked her. I am sure in pre-op not many people thank the anesthesiologist for a great needle stick, but they should.

The intern reviewed the option of general or IV sedation, and I opted for general. Then she told me she hadn't looked at my films, but she didn't recommend general since there was a mass in my mediastinum (the area between the lungs), and when you get general anesthesia, you relax so much that the lesion may press on the aorta and kill you. Cheerful. Maybe I should have just gotten high and refused any anesthetic at all.

Next, I got a shot of heparin, which is a blood thinner. Why? So I didn't throw a clot. No PTT test, which is a way to determine how quickly your blood clots but can also be used to get the dosage of heparin right. No other pre-op blood work at all, actually. Oh, and by the way, I have a history of low platelets, which causes you to bleed out, so it makes perfect sense to give me something that makes it harder for my blood to clot. *Not.* I started to think, *These people are crazy.* Standard of care is like following a textbook called *Surgery for Dummies* that's more about having an excuse if your patient dies than developing the best treatment for that patient. *Ugh.* I let them do it, though. Figured it would be fun for them if they had to end the procedure by scrambling to stop me from bleeding to death through the neck.

Might as well have used the chain saw, in that case.

Actually, I had asked the surgeon, Dr. Portugal, if I could do acupuncture. He said no because he was worried the needles might get in their way during the biopsy. Really? Like, they've got the PICC line in my hand and the EKG leads hanging off my chest, but he thinks a needle in the top of my head will get tangled up while he's excising some tissue? So I opted for IV sedation, which is apparently what they wanted to give me anyway. Besides, I didn't want the twelve-year-old intern to kill me.

As I lay there waiting for them to move me, I thought of the letter in my purse. I'd written it to my kids. Just in case . . . you know. Lori knew it was there.

Next came the resident ear, nose, and throat (ENT) doctor. Why not? Can we get a guy selling popcorn in here, too, while we're at it? This doctor might have been fourteen, give or take a year. I needed to help him palpate my enlarged lymph nodes because he couldn't find the golf ball sticking out of my neck. Maybe if I had pierced it, he would have noticed where it was. Good thing for residencies, because he wasn't ready to do this on his own.

Dr. Portugal entered and told me, "I see you refused the antibiotic." (This is kinda ironic because I do believe that you usually come out of the hospital with more bugs than you go in with. However, antibiotics kill the good bacteria, which fight the bad bacteria. What a dilemma.) "Okay. Today I will be taking the superficial node. That's the one that lies just beneath the skin." (Thus, *superficial*. Sort of.)

"Thanks," I said, "but if you give me *C. diff*, I will kill you." That was about all the mutual respect I could muster at the moment.

C. diff, if you don't know, is a bacterium that causes diarrhea and colitis. It is pretty common to pick up in a hospital. Hospitals are great when you need them, but you're exposing yourself to whatever anybody brought in, and most people coming in have something going on already.

Dr. Portugal smirked in a friendly way, if you can picture that. "You're going to be okay."

I started crying. I hate that kind of statement. No one can guarantee that you will be okay, so don't tell me something you can't guarantee when I'm sitting on your strange bed with a needle in my hand and a team of people in scrubs and masks swarming around me. Say, "I am a great surgeon, and I am going to do my job today. I had a good night's sleep, drank one cup of coffee just in case my cortisol level isn't where it should be, and I am ready to show this fourteen-year-old resident how not to jack up a woman's neck." That's what I wanted to hear.

Down the hall to the operating room was a short ride. They transferred me to another bed in the OR, and that is all I remember.

Two hours later, I was choking. Not sure on what, but all I wanted to do was vomit. I just needed to puke up whatever I was choking on, and I thought I would be fine. Surprisingly, my neck didn't really hurt, but it was very sore.

The incision was *huge*. It went all the way from the front to the back of my neck, and I immediately thought he must have taken the deep one after all. Was that a good or bad thing? I wondered if that one looked worse or better, or if it was just more fun to show the resident. *See, here's how you separate the SCM muscle and carve away at tissue without damaging the jugular vein or the vagus nerve. . . .*

Son of a bitch, playing around in my neck like that.

I had a brief chat with the anesthesiologist. I wanted to know if I said anything funny in the OR. I do love to entertain. She told me I said Dr. Portugal's name and repeatedly asked him not to touch my neck.

"Thank goodness I said *neck* and not something else."

"Oh, we've seen and heard it all," she said. Then she confided in me, "We once had a man in here for a lower-extremity procedure. We gave him the anesthesia, but right there on the table he masturbated to ejaculation."

I don't think she made that up; it's not the kind of thing you tell someone you don't know, but it is the kind of thing you might tell another physician. I could only think I was grateful I didn't touch my vagina so she wouldn't have two of those stories. Would she have told me if I had? Would I have enjoyed the procedure more?

Recovery was monitored by a nurse named Ritchie. He was a DJ by night. Wish he had spun some tunes in post-op, because just lying there is *bor*-ing. Ritchie and I are now Facebook friends. Karen would be so proud of me for that. We used to have contests to see who could get more Facebook friends when we went out. Extra points to me for getting one with my ass hanging out and a neck wound three inches long.

Ritchie gave me a wheelchair ride down to the car for Lori to take me home. Lori and I stopped for lunch on the way. It's not a bad idea to do something seminormal after you've had a piece of your body pulled out through your neck. I still ate well, meaning no sugar, no gluten, and no dairy. We met Lori's husband, Ken, who paid for lunch. Thanks, Ken. Love when the tab gets picked up.

When I got home, Reese and Jackson had made me a huge card with a taco on it. That is a private joke. There were balloons in the walkway and a gluten- and dairy-free cake that was frickin' awesome on the kitchen counter. Ari was out of town. The cake might have come close to my phenomenal gluten-free banana bread in sheer deliciousness. Maybe if I put the recipe in this book, I could sell it to the cooking crowd too.

Friends texted all day to see how I was. I have great friends. I have chosen them well.

Two days later, I was typing in bed at home—resting because I should and not because I wanted to. I don't do rest well. I took a bath, which I don't normally do, and I cried.

January 21, 2014

> *It is easy to be strong when you aren't actually doing anything, but when you're just waiting? I think it will be easier to be brave when I have information. It sucks to wait, to not know what obstacle there is that you want to beat the hell out of until it is gone. What am I fighting against?*
>
> *It is the unknown that scares me because the mind wanders. My right brain gets creative, and my left brain uses logic to get me through the minutes because days don't move fast when there are seven of them between being cut open and being told what that tissue is inside your body taking up space where it doesn't belong.*
>
> *Part of my time capsule was cut out. Part of my heart aches, and part of my brain says,* Stay brave and tough . . . *because that is exactly what I am, and that is how I will walk through cancer.*

10

CANCER CONNECT-THE-DOTS

When you were a child, did you have those coloring books where you had to first connect the dots before you could even see what the picture was to color in? You would start with number one and draw little lines to each subsequent number until you hit the very last one, checking often to see if you could guess the picture. Did you ever try to guess before you started what the picture would look like? How quick were you at figuring it out? Like, could you guess right at about a quarter of the way through? Half? Three-quarters? Or maybe you were the type who reserved judgment until you hit the very last dot?

I never liked not knowing things, so I would guess constantly. Discovering what animal or vehicle or object or character the dots made was not as satisfying for me as predetermining what it was and knowing I was connecting things properly.

Have I mentioned I have control issues?

I'd been playing reverse connect-the-dots. Hodgkin's lymphoma was the last in a series of dots that began with my unexplainable weight gain while training with Lori. There were also the lumps, of course, and the blood work and then the CT scan, but it wasn't until the day the biopsy came back that the whole picture made sense.

Of course, in retrospect, you can trace back to other events that got you to a certain destination. The weight gain might be the first time I knew something was wrong, but the more I think about it, the more I see a long chain of dots going back to my childhood that led me to this point. Working backward, it all made sense.

I was not a breastfed baby, for instance. (I mean, if we're going to go back, let's go all the way back.) There is a lot of research showing how our immune system develops better and stronger when we are breastfed. Of course, babies need to be fed, and sometimes formula is the only option, but evidence does point to the fact that when possible, "the breast is the best."

Much of my childhood is a huge blur, but I know in my teenage years I used to drink Tab for breakfast. There was a time when we thought a soda could be good for us because it had "diet" in the name. Then we started finding out about these food additives people were making in labs and how our bodies process sweeteners, and we came to our senses. Some of us, anyway. Knowing what I know now, I wish I hadn't been throwing all those chemicals into my body every day like that.

I went to college in Arizona. You know what people like to do in Arizona? Suntan. Also known as absorb as much UV radiation as you can. You literally lay out under the sun in as little clothing as possible as if to say, "Here, Sun, give me cancer here, here, here, all over!" To make matters worse, I hadn't gotten as tanned as I wanted before Christmas break my first year, and I couldn't face going home all pasty white, so I did some indoor tanning sessions. That's for people who wish the sun could be pressed against their bodies.

Then I took up pottery as a hobby. I just loved to throw clay. The glazes were lead based, and between breathing that in and the clay dust, I am sure I was introducing plenty of toxins to my system. Four years before my diagnosis, when I would drink any sort of alcohol, and I only needed a few sips, I would get an excruciating pain from the back of my occiput (the back of my skull) into my right trap (all the way to my shoulder blade). It would go away after about twenty minutes as fast as it would arrive. I thought it might be my gallbladder acting up, but nope. I stopped drinking, and the pain went away. Not that I was ever a big drinker, but I used to enjoy an occasional beer or cocktail when I was out to dinner. The pain never returned.

One year prior to my diagnosis, I was in Washington, DC, on a business trip for the American Chiropractic Association. One night, I woke up with bloody feet. The itch was so intense, it was like being bitten by one thousand mosquitoes, but under the skin near the bone where you can't really scratch, so there was no relief. I had scratched so hard in my sleep that I broke the skin on the top of my feet.

Natural or alternative medicine (although it shouldn't be the alternative), which I practice, differs from your standard Western medicine in the way we approach symptom care. Traditional Western medicine, or allopathy, typically uses some form of man-made intervention to deal with a disease or symptoms. Think drugs or surgery. I work with your body's natural ability to heal itself by giving it the right tools. We look for the underlying cause or causes and develop strategies for correcting them with lifestyle changes or using safer, and, in my opinion, better therapies. My approach has also been referred to as functional medicine.

When you visit me, I will probably tell you that your joint pain or your constipation or your cramps during your period are "common, but not normal." Lots of things we treat as "normal" are really common side effects of our Western, industrialized lifestyles. When I work with patients to reduce their exposure to toxins and reduce inflammation caused by poor nutrition, they're surprised that their conditions often clear up without antibiotics or other medications. In functional medicine, I look at you as a whole person, not a fifteen-minute appointment during a busy day. If your doctor makes you feel like a number or doesn't give you resolution, fire them and call me or someone like me. This isn't a sales pitch, I just get worked up when I see how people give up on their health because their doctor can't do more than prescribe something to take the edge off.

Back to what I was trying to say. With most allopathic medicine today, you can find an attitude that we should be able to treat any condition without having to change our behaviors very much. Functional medicine looks at that and says, "Well, shoot, isn't getting an elective surgery or taking drugs your whole life a behavior change? And wouldn't you rather let your body work for itself rather than pump artificial drugs into it?"

It's like that parable people tell about finding bodies floating in a river. Conventional medicine tends to say, "We'd better get these bodies out of the river." Functional medicine says, "What's happening up river that's causing all these bodies to be here?"

I'm oversimplifying, of course. Don't get me wrong (and people get this wrong a lot): I'm not totally against allopathic medicine. There are times when it's the best choice—like when you have Hodgkin's lymphoma and there's an 80 percent chance you'll survive five years with chemotherapy. And good doctors trained in the conventional tradition will often adopt some alternative ways of thinking about causes and treating the patient holistically.

Okay, got that out of the way. Point made: Western medicine is not all bad.

But *chemotherapy*? You're literally injecting poison into your body. On a routine basis. For months. Prior to my diagnosis, you would never have caught me considering chemotherapy. You cannot get further from a natural solution.

The day I was diagnosed with Hodgkin's, when I was feeling particularly alone as a health and wellness practitioner, I called my chiro friend Dr. Michael Taylor. I trust this man with my life. We met decades ago when I was serving as secretary for the American Chiropractic Association Council on Diagnosis and Internal Disorders (try saying that all night when you're introducing yourself at a cocktail party). He was serving as president, so we were co-board members, and we just kind of clicked as professionals and as people. I also happen to admire him because he is brilliant. He practices in Tulsa, a few states away, but we've developed a close friendship with a few states between us.

On the day in question, during work hours if I recall correctly, I called him with the news.

"Oh no, I'm so sorry," he said. "How are you?"

"I don't even know," I told him. "Like, kind of freaked out, I guess. And a bit confused. Like, what do I even do? I need to start hitting this thing with everything I've got. I gotta clean up my diet, maybe look into those alternative treatment centers in Mexico or Germany. My mind won't stop racing."

"Cindy, listen to me," he said in a tone I'd heard him use only when telling stories about talking to his patients. "This thing has a high survival rate with allopathic treatment. You have three kids. You're going to stay here in the United States, and you're going to get chemotherapy, and you're going to be just fine, and you're going to see your children grow up."

I hemmed and hawed for a while, but he kept coming back to the same idea: Stay here. Get chemo. Do it for your kids. Though

I kept resisting and really expected shortly to be on a plane to Germany (they treat patients with cancer very differently—and very successfully—there), in the back of my mind, I knew he was right, and a little voice was saying, *Crap, I'm really going to have to do this.*

Before I hung up, I told him I agreed with him and would follow his advice. Then I sat there at my desk with my phone in my hand and reflected for a long time. For some people, getting chemo is just what you do, no questions asked. For me, though, it required a major mindset shift. I recoiled at the idea of having those toxins swirling around inside me. I imagined with sadness having to admit to my patients that I went the allopathic route. I knew it was for the best, but that didn't mean I had to like it.

Jay, one of the doctors who regularly lectures and the one who can confirm I don't buy my own drinks, is the King of Acronyms. He speaks in them, and it always takes me a minute or two to figure out what he means. Sometimes I don't get it at all. When texting first came out, more acronyms flew over my head. I used to think "LOL" meant "Lots of love." When I looked up "TY" on Urban Dictionary, it said it was the art of extreme masturbation, so I couldn't understand why my daughter would randomly respond with that. Best I could figure, she sent it to me by accident, intending it for a girlfriend or a hot guy. "ROTFL" was a mystery to me for months too.

Have you heard of "ABVD"? Unfortunately, that one became all too familiar way too fast. ABVD stands for a four-drug cocktail that I had to rely on to save my life. There are over 548 approved drugs used for cancer, according to the National Cancer Institute. Four of them are often used for Hodgkin's lymphoma:

A—Adriamycin (doxorubicin hydrochloride)

B—bleomycin

V—vinblastine

D—dacarbazine

These four drugs are from different drug families and are all used to slow or stop the growth of cancerous cells, though in different ways. If you were laying siege to a fortress, you might get farther or at least increase your chances of success by hitting the door with a battering ram, pushing ladders up against the battlements, cutting off the water supply, and tunneling underneath. That's something like what oncologists do with ABVD. We were laying siege to my time capsules.

This is how I view chemo: the act of injecting synthetic drugs into your bloodstream, hoping that these cell assassins don't create too much collateral damage. I already had problems enough with the Hodgkin's lymphoma. Taking the ABVD mix exposed me to the risk of new problems, several of which I actually experienced.

Some of the side effects included increased risk of getting an infection (meaning now I could die of this instead of the lymphoma, which is sometimes how it happens for people); breathlessness and looking pale (as if to directly punish me for the tanning); bruising, bleeding gums, or nosebleeds; and/or tiredness and weakness (essentially, I could go from a bodybuilding contestant to a frail Victorian waif).

I also had to be on the lookout for hypersensitivity reactions, which are different from skin reactions. Then there's the hair loss; I had a plan for that: cold caps. I'll tell you about them later. (Although, I could have lived with never having to shave my legs again. You ever have that thing when you put your leg up on the wall of the shower to shave it, but you got shaving lotion on the bottom

of your foot, so it slides down the wall and you pull your hamstring
catching yourself from slipping and cracking your head open so your
kids don't find you naked and dead an hour later; then you can't put
your leg up to shave for a few weeks, so you're glad it's winter and you
can wear pants? Just me?)

But wait; there's more! Chemo could give me a loss of appetite.
(For Pete's sake: I did not have weight loss with cancer, and I still
didn't with the drugs. That would have at least been an upside. Who
wants to have cancer and not at least lose the last few pounds of
stubborn baby weight?) Maybe mouth sores and ulcers (though that
would never stop me from talking; just ask anyone who has met me).
I was on the lookout for red or pink urine (I thought neon, glow-in-
the-dark pink would be cool, actually); black or brown discoloration
of the skin (I still have some of this on the underside of my arm,
over six years later); reddening of the skin (and not because I'm
blushing after my friend showed me a dick pic from her date last
night); sensitivity to sunlight (would a tanning bed be okay?); and
inflammation around the drip site ("drip site" just sounds gross). To
be honest, so much of this sounded gross, and I don't get squeamish.

There were more possible symptoms—sore eyes, dizziness,
changes of vision, and/or watery eyes. (Ha, I'd been crying already.
I beat them to it.) Periods stopping. (Well, thank goodness. I was
looking forward to this. Update: they came back after a year.
Bummer.) Allergic reactions. (This wasn't fun—and it led to more
drugs. That is the allopathic Circle of Care: Get a symptom -> Take a
drug -> Get a new symptom -> Take a new drug. Why is this a good
idea?) Chemo can cause damage to the heart muscle. (This sucks.)
Numbness or tingling. (They forgot to mention Raynaud's syndrome,
which I have really bad. That's when the blood vessels in your fingers
or toes constrict, and you feel cold and numb.) Inflammation of

the lungs. (This also sucks.) Poop changes (+ or -). Depression, headaches, high temperature and chills, and more.

Out of thirty-four possible side effects, I got six. That is only 17.6 percent. If you want to look at it positively, which I do, it is much better than getting 100 percent.

I liked the prognosis numbers, although I hate statistics. They're very misleading. They can make you feel like you'll certainly be okay, but think about it: if there is even a 1 percent chance a treatment won't work, that means that *someone* has to be that 1 percent. There's no reason to think it couldn't be you, and that would really suck. I went for it anyway. I have three young kids, and I didn't want to die. So far so good.

The ABVD can burn when it goes through the vein, plus if you have the nurse stick you every time in the antecubital fossa (inside of the elbow), they can trash your vein. So, I had a bouncy ball put in the right side of my chest. It is actually called a *port*, but it looked round and stuck out of my chest, and my youngest wanted to know why I had a bouncy ball in my chest, and so that new terminology stuck. I still have a scar there, an indentation and scar tissue, and sometimes it hurts or itches, and sometimes it reminds me how much I went through to get the damn thing removed so we can play jacks with it.

If you aren't very old, you might not know what jacks is. Google will tell you. Jacks was fun. Having a jacks ball in your chest . . . a little less fun. But when you're a kid dancing and running and tanning and throwing back Tab, you can't imagine a time when life won't be as easy as A-B-C, 1-2-3, a time when the picture you get from connecting the dots will be so scary that you'll have to choose between having aliens in your body or welcoming poisons in your veins.

11

DO SOMETHING NEW

FEBRUARY 2, 2014

Sometimes I get disappointed that I don't write things down more often. My brain never stops (kind of like my mouth), and with this whole experience, there are random wild thoughts running through my head all day. I will often have what I think is a hilarious thought in the middle of the day and think, *I should jot that down later.* Only, I don't. As soon as you start imagining an audience, you start obsessing over which details of your life are the important ones, and I want this book to be funny. I mean, it can't be all sad cancer stuff, can it? But I guess if I forget it, it wasn't supposed to be. There are no accidents.

Two days ago, I rode in a helicopter for the first time—that was no accident. I am grateful now because it was my idea, and that's not normally the kind of idea I would have.

I spent the day with Christina. She and I met in chiropractic school, and she is one of a few of our cohort that I have remained close with. When I say *close*, I mean that I can tell her anything—and

I do. She knows many of my secrets and my fears. The fears, I've
learned, diminish when I speak them out loud to someone who does
not judge them. That gives me extra energy, so I can steal the energy
I used to give my fears and pour it into my dreams and goals. Dreams
and goals need energy!

We drove to Sedona for the day because Sedona used to be one
of my favorite places on earth. It has a healing energy, which I know
sounds weird to people, but it's true. Others have experienced it, too,
and a lot of healers will go there on retreats. Now, though, they've put
in a McDonald's and an outlet mall, and while it is still beautiful, it
dropped in my estimation from favorite place on earth.

It makes me sad that we put so much value on material things
that we don't value true beauty in nature. When you look at a
mountain and the terrain of the desert, it moves something inside
you. Then we work so hard to reproduce the colors so we can paint
our kitchen to match some experience, as if it could be reproduced.
On top of that, the actual view gets destroyed because we let
developers block it with chain restaurants and big-box stores.

Untouched nature exhibits such strength and cohesiveness.
When you touch a flower, it dies faster. Why then do we cut them and
put them in vases? They should be left in their natural surroundings
where we can fully appreciate their beauty over their natural lifespan.
We should go to the flowers rather than bring them to us. Maybe then
we'd take better care of the places they like to grow.

But isn't this just like what we do to ourselves that makes us sick?
We alter our environment so drastically that we alter our lives. Maybe we
don't feel it so much in terms of lifespan, as the medical community has
worked so hard to prolong our lives in years, but certainly we feel it in
our habitats and in our quality of life. We spend so much of our lives
in our own little vases, sucking up water, whereas what we really need
is to be rooted back in the earth where we belong.

Our genetic code has what I call light switches. Some are more like a dimmer switch, and when they're on and at the perfect position, the lighting is just right to illuminate what needs to be seen without causing unnecessary shadows or brightness that forces us to squint. When we cut the flower and that flower dies, it is like moving the light switch all the way to off. When the dimmer's not right, we don't function with the innate ability with which we were created. When we cut flowers and put them on our counter to enjoy, they are short lived, and the beauty is no longer there. When we aggravate the cells in our bodies by being too stressed, eating poorly, working around chemicals, etc., they respond by moving that dimmer switch up, thinking the increased light will help us see better. In actuality, that is not true, and we now need sunglasses—which can represent the need for treatment to help us heal after we get sick.

Maximum enjoyment of the flower means letting it grow and develop as it was intended. Maximum enjoyment of our lives means letting our cells keep those dimmer switches at the right levels. Or think of a sound board at a concert. If all those sliders are pushed all the way down, you hear nothing. If they're pushed all the way up, it's cacophony. The best sound requires each slider to be in the right place.

What's that? I was talking about helicopters? Oh, right. So, we got to Sedona, parked on the main drag, and just started walking down the strip of shops. We got barely one hundred yards before we ran into this helicopter tour kiosk, and Christina asked the gentleman running it for a recommendation for a good place to eat. It is amazing what people assume is good; a place with *pizza* in the name was not what we were looking for. But he was kind, and I started to inquire about the helicopter tour. He explained there were three different tours at three different prices: Tour A, Tour B, or Tour C, which was a combination of both Tours A and B. You picked your tour; then they weighed you to figure out where to seat you, because helicopters are all about weight and balance, and so on.

I looked at Christina like, *Should we do this?*

She didn't even hesitate. "I am in!" she said.

I started thinking, *I don't like to fly. I don't want to die. But, on the other hand, I'm not with my kids.*

I do believe in trying new things and experiencing life, but I'm not generally a big thrill seeker. We should be able to choose the level of experiencing life we're comfortable with. Experiencing cancer hasn't made me more reckless, as if I don't care whether I die or not. I do not want to die, nor did I plan to let this cancer kill me. But something that day just said, *Do it.*

What the kids not being there had to do with it, I don't know. I guess I was thinking it would be better if they didn't witness me dying in a horrible helicopter crash. Or if the universe was going to judge me for doing something stupid, like go up in a helicopter as a single parent of three kids, at least I didn't take them out with me.

"Okay, me too," I said. Then I asked, "Could you give us Tour C for the Tour B price?" and I threw in, "I'll let you weigh me in naked," like I was a co-ed on spring break. I'm not ashamed of my body or that modest, but I don't normally offer to disrobe for a deal. Anyway, he agreed to the lower fare, but the girl who weighed me in wasn't interested in me naked, so I didn't actually have to follow through on that part.

While we were completing our booking and getting weighed in and all, I leafed through one of the magazines they had on the table. Of course, some of them were helicopter magazines, and one of them had a story about . . . you guessed it, *a helicopter crash.*

"Why the fuck are we doing this, again?" I asked Christina, showing her the article.

"Because it's something we've never done before and may never get a chance to do again," she said. "Besides, statistically speaking, if there was a recent crash, we aren't due for another one for a long time."

I know enough about statistics to know that's a load of crap, but I also reserve the right to believe whatever load of crap I need to believe to get my ass onto a helicopter.

They placed me in the front seat, which, it turns out, is the best seat. The bottom was made of glass (or plexiglass, or whatever. It was clear.). I could look ahead of me, to the sides, and straight below. We don't always get to look at the world literally under our feet like that. It was like seeing where I'm going, where I could go, and where I was right then, all at the same time.

I always want the best seat from now on. Why not? Living life from the rear seat is too bumpy. The middle seat can zap my energy from all angles, causes motion sickness like chemo nausea, and has a crummy view. The front seat gives me an opportunity to see exactly where I am going and to get excited about what lies ahead.

The tour took us through the mountains at what felt like an absurdly low altitude. It even occurred to me we might have a chance of surviving a crash if we were this low and didn't have far to fall. Whether we'd be rescued before bleeding out all over the mountainside was another matter. Seeing the mountains from the eagle's perspective takes your breath away. You feel like you could reach out and squeeze the forests, and when you pass through a narrow canyon over a river, you feel a surprising connection to it all, like you belong there and it's holding you up.

If anything, it was way too short, afraid as I was. The first couple minutes you spend just getting used to it and thinking, *I'm going to die; I'm going to die.* Then you begin to accept your reality: *If I'm going to die, I'm going to die, and there's nothing much I can do about it now.* When you don't, in fact, immediately run into an avalanche on the side of the mountain, you start to realize how amazing it all is. And about that time, they turn around and take you back down.

But it was so worth it.

I expected to have a lot of health and nutrition advice in this book, but here and now I recommend a helicopter ride. Here is why: You will see a view of nature that most people will never ever see, and even if you repeat the experience, it will be different. It is impossible to fly the exact pattern in the exact weather at the exact height with the exact people on the exact day ever again. How unique is that? What a gift it is to have a moment in time that is so beautiful, it touches your soul. Cancer gave that to me, in a way, or at least I wasn't going to let cancer take it from me.

Go do something scary like ride in a helicopter. Make your own beautiful moment. Get lost in it, and make it part of your energy terrain. There's a new term for you: *energy terrain.* If you imagine your soul like a landscape—whatever landscape comes to mind—your energy terrain is where you can go inside yourself to draw energy. There are hopefully a few if not lots, and every new experience offers the promise of adding to them—or taking them away. Every day I want the gift of even the briefest experience of altering my terrain in a positive way.

Yesterday, it was an old friend who altered my terrain. Nick reached out to me. He is one of my favorite people from high school, and we have this energetic connection without a lot of effort and without having to be physically in the room. In his kind words, I found inspiration, and that inspiration got me thinking.

When you get diagnosed with something that other people find scary, it is amazing how people extend offers or inspiration or advice.

You become the focus of that friendship, which is lovely, but I have heard people minimize their own importance and the importance of their own battles. That's not what I want at all. If you're my friend and I get sick, you become even more important to me. I want to be a better friend than ever, a rock when someone needs it, a source of laughter (when appropriate), and an inspiration if necessary. I am now reaching out to others to let them know that I am here in any capacity they need. Yes, I need some things from some people, but I also want to still be there for you. I love you, friends.

I have a PET scan tomorrow; I will know more about my time capsules. I am not yet sure how I feel about that.

I visited with my mother this weekend. I will not see her again for six months, as neither of us will be able to travel. I am sad. Let's leave it at that.

I'm doing all I can, spinning in circles until the Wonder Woman costume appears so that I can supercharge.

12

THE TWO-MARTINI ACCIDENT

For a long time, I planned to title this book *Pregnancy Is Worse Than Cancer*. If you hadn't noticed yet, I tend to speak my mind. Also, I either have no filter or it's broken. Sometimes I put things in ways that rub people the wrong way. That's why I keep my feet as clean as possible and my toes well manicured—they end up in my mouth so often.

This title came to me when I first started treatment back in March 2014. I ran it past Spencer, and he said, "That's it!" When you have a Spencer in your life and he tells you he loves your title, you're going to love that title too.

Remember, also, that was a complicated time of my life. I had doubled down on the things I knew were best for me: eating well, exercising like a maniac, spending time with friends and family. Team Winning! was doing well, but it was a lot of work. Keeping track of your supplements, meds, and appointments and the simple fact of being aware of this thing in your body take a lot of bandwidth even on the days you're feeling well.

Here's what I wrote at the time:

Pregnancy is worse than cancer. For real. In my forty-five short years on this earth, I can tell you that my three pregnancies were worse than my cancer. The end results of them all were fantastic, of course—and I mean all four events. I have three beautiful, amazing, smart, funny, joyful, outrageous kids that I adore but can't wait to get out of my house. And I am alive. Because I am alive, I get to enjoy Reese, Ari, and Jackson. For all four events, then, I am grateful.

I can tell you with 100 percent certainty that I would not trade any one of these four crises for anything else if I could go back in time. They are gifts. I honestly believe that. The fact that they were all bad does not mean that they were all bad in the same way, and as I consider the situation, I have to conclude pregnancy was worse than cancer.

Let's look at the evidence [as experienced by me; others may not agree at all, and that's okay]:

- *I threw up every time I ate during pregnancy. During cancer . . . no vomiting.*
- *I can tell you nothing tasted good the second time around or coming up through my nose. With chemo, food had no real taste, and it didn't take that return trip through my nose. I'll admit I'm no foodie, so maybe this is just me, but I'd rather not taste my food at all than have to vomit it up.*
- *Over all three pregnancies, I gained a total of 106 pounds. Steroids with chemo: twelve pounds total. Pregnancy wins again. Or is it cancer that "wins"? You know what I mean.*

- *With pregnancy, I got to buy really bad overalls that hugged my belly but were tight in the crotch. With chemo, my butt and legs got smaller, so I treated myself to new True Religion and Rock & Republic jeans. So fun.*
- *While pregnant, I was tired all the time but couldn't sleep well. With chemo, I was tired for only three or four days every two weeks.*
- *When I was pregnant, everyone told me that I looked great— but I didn't. When I had cancer, everyone told me I looked great, and I did.*
- *When I was pregnant, my breasts grew as big as watermelons. With cancer they did not change. That one is a toss-up, I suppose, depending on whom you ask. I'm sure there are men out there thinking,* What's wrong with breasts as big as watermelons? *I don't know. Why don't you try growing some and see how you like it?*
- *My first pregnancy lasted six and a half months; the next was nine months, and then the third was nine more. That's twenty-four and a half months of my life with swollen feet, an aching back, and bad overalls. Cancer took six months of my life.*
- *Pregnancy led to years of poopy diapers. Cancer? One week of urinary incontinence that, while, let's be honest, was very unpleasant, was at least an easy fix.*

　　So, Your Honor, on these grounds, I submit that pregnancy is definitely worse than cancer.

A decent case when you put it that way, right? Then, as I was putting this book together in 2020, I started telling more people about it. One night, I shared it with my friends Kathy and Wendy over a couple bottles of wine. Their friend Julie was there too. Julie, it turned out, had breast cancer twenty years ago in her thirties. So, I told them all about the book and how my ghostwriter hated the title but that I loved it. (My ghostwriter later insisted he had only suggested I "rethink" the title, but I know what he meant.)

Well, the night progressed with more chatter and wine (I was drinking water). I shared more parts of the book, and then I asked them what they thought, specifically, about the title. I wish I could say I was prepared for what they said. Julie, who had had plenty to drink by this point, leaned forward and started calling me out.

"You know; it's funny," she said. "Earlier you said your ghostwriter wanted to know if you were always so positive, and when I first heard the title, I thought the same thing. Like, *Is she really this positive?* But then I thought, *No, this is bullshit.*

"I kept a cancer journal too. Every day, I was writing it all down, and you know what? I threw it all out. When it was all over, and I looked back through it, I had to get rid of it. Every day was another terrible thing. It was all about how horrible the experience was. It sucked, and I was miserable, and I hated it.

"And here you're laughing and saying, 'Oh, I'd rather have cancer than get pregnant again,' and it's making me feel upset and depressed because there was nothing positive that I saw through my experience. Nothing. So what does that mean? Am I weak? Or is cancer really horrible, and you're full of shit?"

It was a lot to process, of course, but I actually appreciate people who can be direct with me like that. I wasn't offended, though it wasn't what I wanted to hear. Keeping calm as best I could, I said, "You know, that's really helpful, to hear your experience. I'm sorry it was so bad for you, and of course I can't change your experience. Honestly, though, I'm sad for you that you threw those journals out.

Even if they're all about bad stuff, they're still a record of what you were feeling during that time.

"Maybe that title is more a chapter than the book title," I acknowledged. "Because, for me, if I had to choose to do one again, pregnancy or cancer, I'd honestly choose cancer."

"What, did you almost die when you were pregnant?" Julie shot back.

"As a matter of fact, yes."

It was late fall of 2001, almost two years after Steve and I got married, and we were partying at some bar for some reason, and I'd had two martinis. Turns out that's how many martinis it takes to make me climb onto the bar and start dancing. I know I had martini three in my hand because I was bummed I couldn't finish it when Steve said, "Let's go home."

Only he said it in that way that means, "Let's go home because what I want to do to you isn't decent to do in company."

Come to think of it, that's not the way Steve usually said things. I should have asked how many martinis *he'd* had.

You need to understand something about me, and I don't think it's going to surprise you: I was not into getting pregnant. Even when I was young, I never wanted kids. I used to think, *This world is a pretty shitty place. I don't know if I want to bring kids into all this.* Steve wanted kids because that was what you were supposed to do, but I hadn't been convinced yet.

In other words, we were not "trying." Thus, I call Reese "my Two-Martini Accident." One martini less and I might have fought to stay. One more and I would have passed out before anything could happen.

I didn't want a pregnancy, and pregnancy didn't seem to want me. I was nauseated. *A lot.* Like I said, vomiting pretty much every time I ate. I started to joke that I was getting good at knowing which foods came up well and which didn't, which ones would come through your nose and which would get stuck in your throat. "I could write a book on bulimia," I joked. (Too dark for you? I think that's about as dark as I'll get.) I had retrosternal pain ("behind the sternum") that the nurse-midwife thought was heartburn or a gallbladder issue. I would take my blood pressure, and it would be 120/80, which is normal according to the textbooks but high for me. My normal is 110/72. I kept telling people something was wrong, but they kept assuring me it was all going to be fine. (See a pattern here?)

As horrible as I felt, I did want a nice experience. I saw a nurse-midwife because they tend to treat pregnancy as a natural bodily function rather than a medical emergency. I came up with this whole birth plan for what we were going to bring to the hospital, how I wanted to deliver the baby, what music we were going to play. I really started to get into it. I became that mom-to-be going around asking, "Do you think I should bear down to Mozart's 'A Little Night Music' or 'Crazy Train' by Ozzy Osbourne?"

We were up in Wisconsin on Mother's Day weekend of 2002. My due date was July 23, so I was well on the way, but although I had gained only twenty-six pounds, I was swollen up like I was three hundred. The only time I felt okay was in water, so I spent most of Mother's Day in the tub. When we got back to Chicago, I wasn't feeling so hot. That Monday, I went to work but felt so bad, I came home early—which I *never* do. My massage therapist came to the house to work on me, but I kept feeling worse. The next morning, I got a bloody nose that just wouldn't stop. I still have the blood-spattered pajamas. Why? Probably for the same reason I have a cabinet full of broken pots that I created (more on this later).

I took my blood pressure: 190/110. If you don't know, that is very high, like call-your-doctor-you-have-hypertension high. So, I called the midwife's office and spoke to a nurse. I said, "My blood pressure is 190/110, and I'm bleeding to death." She said, "It's probably just your elevated liver enzymes. You'll be fine."

I still haven't forgotten that nurse.

Now, I don't do doctors or hospitals. I'd rather die at home, thank you very much. But there was a baby involved, and I knew that nurse was full of shit and something was wrong. So I called Steve and told him he'd better take me to the hospital.

My water broke on the way. When I got there, they hooked me up to all the machines and got an IV in me. They ran my blood and got a platelet count of 30,000. In my office, I consider a normal count between 150,000 and 450,000. They strapped me onto the bed because they were worried I would have a seizure. Low platelets cause problems with not being able to form blood clots, so bleeding is a concern, not seizures, but you can't reason with these people, and I was delirious, so nothing made sense.

This was Silver Cross in Joliet, Illinois, a Level 2 hospital. If I had had the baby there, they would have sent her to RUSH University Medical Center, a Level 3 hospital, for care. But I would have been stuck recovering at Silver Cross. So, they loaded me into an ambulance and shipped me over to RUSH, about forty-five minutes away, so I could be admitted to the same place as my baby.

It was around 10:00 p.m. at this point, and a nurse and a resident rode in the ambulance with me. The nurse talked to me about kids and baseball and whatever just to keep me occupied, but the resident kept falling asleep and getting jostled awake. At one point I asked the nurse, "Hey, is she going to be okay?" The nurse just gave me a look that said she didn't want to talk about it.

I remember having contractions in my butt—at least, that's what it felt like. I never had abdominal contractions like you're supposed to. The whole time I was still bleeding, but despite my discomfort, I felt very distracted by everything happening around me.

Like, at the hospital they said they were going to have to "pull the baby," meaning a C-section. I could only think, *I hope it's a girl. Please be a girl.* Girls' lungs develop more quickly. This baby was going to be born two months early; I wanted it to have the best chance possible of making it, so in my mind, that meant it was important it be a girl.

The next thing I thought was, *Wait, what about the birth plan? I have this whole plan!* There was supposed to be music, and my mom was going to be there. A C-section was the thing I had worked so hard to avoid this whole pregnancy. My mom and dad made it to the hospital, but they had to stay with Steve in the waiting room. And where was Ozzy? Why wasn't I on the crazy train right now?

They put me on a bed and began to wheel me down to the OR. One of the nurses or the anesthesiologist (again, delirious) was this rather fit young guy. I'm about to have my baby prematurely pulled out of my body through a hole in my stomach, and I'm thinking, *Wow, that guy is gorgeous.* Then I said, "Are you guys going to have to shave me?" It dawned on me, looking at the hot nurse, that I hadn't had a Brazilian wax in ages. After all, who can see their labia when they're seven months pregnant? I was thinking that the hot nurse would have to shave me for an emergency C-section. I was mortified.

There was a lot of activity as people attached things to me and began the procedure. The resident said they were going to do "an old-fashioned C-section," meaning a vertical incision starting at my belly button instead of the horizontal one. There was less risk of my bleeding out that way, he said. He didn't mention that I'd have this silly vertical scar on my stomach that would make it look like I have a second ass in the front.

In a routine C-section, they put the baby up to your breasts and let you start nursing and bonding right away. When the baby is only twenty-nine and a half weeks old, they cart the poor thing away to the neonatal intensive care unit immediately and then wheel the mother to a recovery room. I have a vague memory of someone saying it was a boy.

Except it was a girl. Reese Haley, two pounds seven ounces, and thirteen inches. The official diagnosis was HELLP syndrome and preeclampsia, a pregnancy-related condition in which your blood pressure goes up and you now have protein in your urine, and I don't mean a little extra chicken. HELLP stands for hemolysis (breakdown of red blood cells), elevated liver enzymes, and low platelets, and it's fatal for the mother something like 30 percent of the time, and it can be fatal for the babies who are too premature to survive. In other words, I was lucky. We were lucky. Of course, if they had listened to me, they would have caught it earlier, and I wouldn't have needed so much luck.

They kept Reese in one of those plastic NICU incubators for seven weeks. Her poor, tiny, fragile body had a tube going down her throat and another in her chest. For five days, they kept her on the respirator to make sure she got enough oxygen and to help promote her lung development. Her lungs were underdeveloped, but, boy, her bowels worked well. She would have a blowout all across the incubator, spraying the walls so bad, the nurse would have to order a clean one and, I assume, incinerate the old one. (Reese, I love you, honey!) I would spend sixteen to twenty hours each day in there with her, talking to her and touching her. I'd pump so she could get real breast milk through her feeding tube. I would hold her skin against my skin, which at the time they called kangarooing. I didn't go to work, didn't pay any bills (which, by the way, did not make them disappear), didn't return any phone calls. I was just there for Reese. The most important thing to me was that someone be with her as she fought to stay in this world.

The funny thing is I didn't get angry or depressed about it. I didn't think, *Dammit, this is exactly the kind of shitty thing I didn't want to happen*. This was my little girl, and I was going to be there for her, and that was it.

She never cried for five days. I didn't know what to make of that. She would fuss and fidget, but she didn't cry. She couldn't, I suppose, because of the breathing tube, and part of me wanted nothing more than to hear her cry. Like a normal, healthy baby.

Reese grew up small but tough, and she has no fear. I have no doubts that the nurses at RUSH and the allopathic care we received there saved our lives. I tell people that if I won $20 million in the lottery, the first thing I'd buy is a '69 red Corvette convertible (which I fell in love with before Prince wrote a song about it), but the truth is I would first call the NICU at RUSH and ask what they needed, anything, and buy that first.

To this day, whenever I hear a baby cry, my heart lifts at the sound of life. Even on an airplane, it makes me happy, reminds me that my little girl made it.

To be fair, the other pregnancies were nowhere near as traumatizing. But Ari was born premature too. Just a couple weeks, so he came out at six pounds. C-section again. After my water broke, I never felt contractions. We tried to stimulate labor with acupuncture, but nothing was happening, and then the baby's oxygen level started to drop. The nurse-midwife said, "Here's the deal: you can either consent to the C-section, or you can check yourself out and drive out to RUSH University Medical Center for Pitocin (a drug used to induce labor) to see if that gets things going."

My husband looked at me and said, "Please consent to the C-section. Let's make sure you're both all right." So, a second C-section, a second premature delivery. I was 0 for 2 having anything like the peaceful, natural birth I had wanted. Was it because I hadn't secured the rights to "Crazy Train" from Ozzy? It was the right choice, though: They found out the cord had been wrapped around his neck. He was born healthy, but we could have lost him.

Yet I was dumb enough to get pregnant a third time. Here's the thing: I actually really love my kids. It sounds silly to say that, but I didn't know before I had Reese that I was going to like being a parent. So, there I was about to have a third baby.

With this one, I was dead set on VBAC-ing this baby (vaginal birth after Cesarean). It's even more common now than it was back then; something like 70 percent of women who try it succeed. I took care of myself to keep my blood levels healthy and strong, and I told the nurse-midwife in no uncertain terms that things were going to go down like I had planned this time. She said if I dilated to eight or nine centimeters, she'd proceed with a VBAC. I said, "You're pulling this baby out of my vagina."

Not long before my due date, my nurse-midwife told me she was having knee surgery on a certain date. "So, whatever you do, don't go into labor this weekend," she joked.

You can see where this is going. That weekend, I started to leak amniotic fluid. I knew exactly what it was, but for some reason I just joked that I was peeing myself. There's some concern for infection and for increased problems during delivery when you have a leak this late, so usually they try to induce. Me? I knew I wasn't supposed to have the baby until Monday, so I went about my business. Sometimes knowing exactly what is going on can make you even dumber.

Monday morning, I called the midwife and said I needed to come in and have them strip the membranes (of the amniotic sac) to get this labor started. The midwife said she was still out and that I needed to go to the obstetrician she worked under. I knew if I went to him, he was going to schedule a C-section so that he could get home for dinner on time, so I tried to sabotage him by having a good breakfast before I went. No dice. They sent me home, told me to fast all day and to come back in the evening for a C-section. Jackson was a whopping six pounds, seven ounces. He still holds the prize for my heaviest newborn, and with all of them coming in under six and a half pounds, I still get wide-eyed whenever someone has an eight-pound baby. Looks more like a four-month-old to me.

I didn't unload all of that on poor Julie, but I gave her enough to get the gist and to justify my apparently cavalier attitude about cancer.

Wendy chimed in around this time, though, and said, "Okay, but if you really want to use that title, you have to make it about your truth, because it is your truth, but like Julie's saying, a lot of people who have been through cancer are going to get pissed and feel like you're belittling their experience."

And she was right, for which I am grateful. You can't go around acting like your experience is how everyone should feel, even if you wish they could. Which I do. So here I am six years later still learning from this whole experience.

But can you believe I wanted a fourth kid? After three rough pregnancies. Except, I didn't want three boys in a row. That would create a middle child, and there are so many nightmare therapy stories about middle children. I didn't want another girl, either. You know the saying that G-d gives you only what you can handle? I could hardly handle one. So, no boy and no girl, and they said those were really the main options. Steve and I didn't exactly try, but we didn't *not try* either. I guess it wasn't in the cards.

The kids' takeaway from all this is that when I tell their birth stories, I have to say they came out of my stomach. They're happy I don't have to say "my vagina."

Come here, kids. *Vagina. Vagina vagina vagina!*

13

MY FIRST CANCER FRIEND

In February, I made my first cancer friend. How ridiculous does that sound? Especially from someone so intent on not being defined by cancer.

I drove almost two hours in traffic to the Block Center for Integrative Cancer Treatment in Skokie for my appointment with Dr. Keith I. Block. He is famous because he wrote a book. Hey, *I'm* writing a book. I will be famous too. His book is called *Life over Cancer*, and when I'm past all this, you'll have at least one good reason to think he knows what he's talking about.

Today my pulse was too high: 96. As was my blood pressure: 136/79. No one seems to care, probably because anything short of a full-on panic attack is going to be normal when you're dealing with cancer.

They took fifteen tubes of blood. I said, "What are you, my ex-husband?" Ah, good times at the oncologist's. Dr. Block spent a lot of time with me, which I respect since it's something I value doing for my own patients. He looked at my supplement list and ripped it apart, crossing off most of the items and replacing them with his preferred brands. Some he was okay with. He handed me back the list. I looked it over, and then I crossed out a couple of his. Only fair, right? It must be a joy to have another medical professional as a patient.

This center was more what I was looking for. Chemo with vitamin C before and after with a glutathione push. What's the big deal about vitamin C? Only that it has been shown to minimize pain and reduce toxicity in cells of chemotherapy patients. In other words, offering vitamin C meant they were not just trying to bomb the cancer; they were helping my body fight it naturally. I wanted to help myself stay alive with natural treatment while the necessary chemo was poisoning me. This center, which would counter chemical warfare with natural remedies, would allow exactly that.

While I was waiting for Dr. Block, I met Samantha. Breast cancer survivor. Twice. She was here for a nutrition consultation so she would never get it again. She struck up a conversation immediately with me, and all we talked about was treatments. I decided I was going to change that. When I met people at these centers, I would ask them about their favorite game or if they liked roller coasters or Zac Efron. There was so much more to talk about than cancer and treatment and why we got it. Zac Efron alone could sustain a friendship for several years. Samantha was sweet. I wished her good luck. I also wished I were wishing her luck at the casino. That would have felt more fun.

February 10, 2014

> *It dawns on me that I have a lot of friends. I truly think I have a lot of good friends. I have two great friends. I am grateful for all of them. Yet, I am so lonely. . . .*

Isn't that fascinating? It dawned on me earlier this week that I am lonely, and it is not for a lack of people in my life. It's got me really upset. I am not sure if most people will understand what I mean by this, but a few of you will. I am lonely in this journey because no one walks my walk and no one has the same experience and no one can see the pain inside. There is something about this diagnosis that creates moments of extreme loneliness. It passes quickly, but there are bouts of it just about every day. At these times, there is no one I want to talk to, no one I want to be around, and no one who can relate to my journey. I have also discovered that I am already tired of trying to convince everyone that I am fine and that I will conquer this with such enthusiasm and positivity. People expect a whole lot less. I don't. Never have, never will.

Celeste is my therapist. She also reads my charts and confirms that when my life is more chaotic than usual and communication is a challenge, it is always due to Mercury being in retrograde. I like to blame things on retrograde when I do not assume personal responsibility. I blame Bill Clinton for feeling that way; he should have just owned up to that blowjob.

After I met Samantha, my first cancer friend, Celeste and I talked about the loneliness I had been feeling. Celeste closed her eyes for a moment and declared that she saw what was happening. People in my life have always seen me as strong, always in control, and always successful. She saw them being afraid that I might be weak or that I might struggle through this. That was interesting because I didn't feel that was an option.

She explained that people don't know what to do most of the time—with me and my diagnosis, that is. Sometimes, I would teach them. I would tell them exactly what I wanted them to say or do for me or what I didn't need from them. Other times, I just didn't want to because I would rather put my efforts elsewhere. That's part of the loneliness, too—feeling like you have to educate everyone in how to be your friend when you have this diagnosis. Sometimes, you just want people to know what to do so you can feel free to be yourself.

Dr. Block took me off all animal protein but fish. Ugh, I would miss my red meat. He also wanted no coconut oil; not sure I agreed with that. He told me to eat melons, which I totally disagreed with; too moldy, ew. He said only egg whites. Okay. Lots of nuts, seeds, and legumes. Agreed. Berries, leafy green veg, and a ton of veggies, in general. Got it.

Tea . . . can do.

Soy . . . no problem. (But how do I get it not genetically modified, which 95 percent of the market is, and therefore not healthy?)

Tart cherry juice . . . I use that for arthritis, but okay.

Lots of cabbage juice . . . Lots of what now? I didn't even know that was a thing. Have you ever *seen* a cabbage? Not exactly the kind of thing you look at and, go, "Bet I could juice that." *All right, all right*, I thought, *I'll try it, but I'm going to have to work into that one.*

He insisted I keep my room dark at night so as not to disturb my melatonin. I honestly didn't think that was an issue, but I made a note to check it anyway. He was so big on this melatonin thing that he suggested I use a red light in the bathroom at night so I would be exposed to no blue light at all during sleeping hours, because blue light reduces melatonin levels. I assured him I can and do pee in the dark. I guess he didn't exactly ask for that information, but I've got my pride, haven't I? Hadn't missed the toilet yet and didn't plan to. It's a gift, I know. I leave the whole "urinate all over the seat, walls, bathtub, door, and ceiling" thing to my boys.

Okay, real talk: The opening to the toilet, even with the seat down, has to be at least one thousand times larger in diameter than the hole in the penis. How is it that the urine can't make it into the toilet? The penis is even moveable, so you can aim it. We all know that boys are used to holding it and swinging it around. Can you just point and shoot for the twenty seconds it takes you to pee?

Rant over.

I had a sweet potato for dinner. Decided to add some quinoa and broccoli to the mix next time. We are going to talk a lot about food: Why, how much, new recipes, etc. Considered trying my banana bread with zucchini and egg whites. Guess that would make it "white" zucchini bread. Don't steal that idea. If it works, I am selling the concept to Lettuce Entertain You. That should make me about ten bucks, and I can buy more egg whites to make more white zucchini bread.

> *That is one of my new goals. I will try new food combinations until it gets exciting. We shall see how that goes.*
>
> *Today was a great day. I got more information, and more information is a fabulous thing. A few more appointments to go, and the real ride begins.*

By the way, I refuse to keep my arms and legs inside at all times. I just don't follow the rules, so save your breath and let me wave them around and be obnoxious. I'm walking through cancer over here.

Sweet dreams tonight.

14

WHY I GOT DIVORCED DURING CHEMOTHERAPY

"So, does the cancer change anything with you and Steve?"

Lori and I were standing in her kitchen drinking tea and talking about treatment and training and this and that. We could talk about almost anything.

"About the divorce?" I said.

"Yeah. Like, does this change your mind at all, make you want to work harder to reconcile?"

"Absolutely not," I said before I even gave the question any thought. I knew in my gut that divorce was still the right thing. And I said this, knowing that other friends of mine had had rough periods in their marriages and decided to stick it out. Whenever I pictured the course of my treatment, though, Steve was never there. There was a big blank where he should have been. I knew him too well to believe that he could step up and be what I needed through this.

Lori, like most of my friends, thought I was nuts to get divorced in the first place. Nor was she alone in thinking I was even more nuts for pushing on with it after I was diagnosed with cancer.

Hey, I'm Wonder Woman. I got this. I didn't ask for any of this, but I got it.

So, okay, my ex-husband, Steve, gets one chapter of my book. Honestly, he's lucky to get that much, but I feel like I need to explain why he's not in most of the book despite our not finalizing the divorce until two years after these events. (Yes, it really took that long. The judicial system sucks.) I hope I'm not spiteful about him in these pages. Most of the time, when I think about him and our marriage, I feel sad rather than bitter. It could have been different. There were a lot of good things about it. I wanted so bad for it to work.

But it didn't.

Let me try to encapsulate my experience of being married to Steve. The day I got my diagnosis, we met for coffee at a Starbucks. I can still picture the table by the window where we sat and which chairs we were in. I had a tea and he had a coffee. Things had been pretty rough with us for a while already. In fact, I'd tried to kick him out a couple times but felt sorry for him when he couldn't find a job or a new place, and would let him back in. When I said, "I do," I thought that I meant forever, but I was so stifled and exhausted by the whole thing at that point, I felt divorce was the right option.

We were sitting there talking about whatever from our day, and finally I said:

"I have to tell you something. I've got this lump here, right? I did a CT scan on it and got the results back today. It's cancer. I don't know what kind yet, or how bad, but it's cancer."

He looked stoical. I thought I had gotten used to his apathy, but this night it irritated me. He didn't seem to feel the impact of what I'd said, which felt like he didn't care about my health or me.

"Have you told the kids?" he asked, and I'm sure I gave him a quizzical look. It's not that I was withholding anything from them, but I didn't understand why that was the first thing on his mind.

"No, not yet," I replied.

"Well, if you're not going to tell them, I'll tell them," he said. And just like that, we were in another fight.

"It's not about not telling them; I thought I'd tell you first, is all."

"It's all right," he said. "I'll do it." He kept sipping at his drink like this was a casual, friendly talk. It was as if he were saying he would get the kids a pizza (more junk food) for dinner because he wanted a pizza that night; he thought he was being Super Dad, but it wasn't the kind of help I wanted or needed.

"It's not really your news to tell," I explained. "It's mine, and I get to do it in my own way, in my own time, and I will. Why are we even arguing about this?"

But I knew why. Everything with him was about an exchange of power. He always had to feel like he had something over me. He couldn't feel happy for me when good things happened to me or I succeeded at something, and he rarely appeared to care when anything bad happened. His career never went as well as mine, and best I could tell, he thought my doing well made him look bad.

When I got my diagnosis, his primary concern was how great an inconvenience it might be to him. No, "Wow, I'm so sorry. How can I help?" No, "Hey, we'll get through this." This is a guy who already knew his marriage was on the rocks, and here's a situation where he could prove himself, and his response is, "Well, I'm going take this from you and tell the kids." That's why Lori drove me to my appointments, or I drove myself. That's why I never considered him part of my team. It was like, "Hey, tough luck, but this is your thing." The one time I asked him to do something for my first chemo treatment, you wouldn't believe the fit he pitched. Sure, there were times when I wondered if I could go through a divorce at the same

time as cancer, but then something like that would happen and the
decision once again was clear.

We met in chiropractic school in the 1990s. Even now, if you met
him, you'd think he was charming. Everyone thinks he's charming.
And he is, if he's in class or playing basketball or at a party. They
don't see what happens when he goes home at the end of the day.
That's when you see that the charm is his way of keeping friends
in his life but keeping them at a comfortable distance. He was very
difficult to get close to. The problem was never abusive treatment; it
was negligence. Some days he just felt like a big emotional black hole
moving through our house.

Of course, there were warning signs. There are always warning
signs. But I didn't want to see them at the time. We were supposed to
be in love, after all. I know exactly why I fell in love with him. When
we met, I had just come out of an abusive, controlling relationship—
the kind where he wants to know why you're late and where you've
been and whom you were with. It was suffocating. Steve was the exact
opposite. Quiet, chill, easygoing. I could come home late from work
three days in a row, and he wouldn't say a thing. He all but told me,
"I don't give a shit that you're late; do whatever you want to do." I was
too naive or wounded to see that it wasn't about being laid back; it
was a near-total lack of emotional connection. Emotional negligence
can be just as suffocating as abuse, only in a different way. It took me
a while to see that I wanted something in between, a third way. Like,
if you love someone, you should be interested enough in their day or
what they're doing to at least ask after them. It doesn't have to be a
choice between apathy and the third degree. But at the time, I was so

sensitive to any signs of his being controlling that I didn't even think about the other kind of problem.

We were best together when nothing much was required of him. Going out for dinner and a movie. Staying home to watch a movie. Maybe going for a walk with the dog. Then the kids came along. He was attentive enough, but I started to notice a pattern that had been there all along. I was carrying the whole marriage. The more kids we brought home, the more I noticed I was carrying the whole family. I set all our priorities; I made all the decisions; I was the strong one when someone needed something. If we went on a trip, I would do all the planning. He had trouble getting his career off the ground, so I made most of the money too.

It's funny, but looking back on our marriage, I see myself playing both traditional parts, the husband and the wife. Make the money, raise the kids, plan the trips, clean the house. I pretty much did it all, and he came along for the ride. Or didn't. I was our social manager too. Once we got married, he suddenly didn't want to see our friends anymore. He'd always try to get out of going to parties with me, and then when we got there, he'd be angling to go home early.

To me, anyway. To everyone else, he was charming, friendly Steve, the guy I had originally fallen for. That's probably why people had such a hard time understanding my decision.

Part of me feels like I came on too strong. Like, maybe I didn't really give him the chance to step up and be everything he could be because I just charged in and did it myself. Ironically, I got that from my dad. He's always been a strong man, and I take after him in a lot of ways. Instead of looking for a husband who was like him, I began to act like him inside my own marriage.

It took me a long time to come to the decision to share a life with Steve. I mean, I wasn't even sure I was going to get married, much less have kids. But when I stood up under the chuppah at the country club and made my vows, I really meant them. I was making a lifelong commitment, do or die, sickness or health. And if I promise you something, I don't go back on it. I'm good for it. As much as there were signs of unpleasantness in our marriage, I never thought of walking away. Certainly not of cheating on him. But as I told my friend Kristin, the sad thing is that if I had cheated on him, he probably wouldn't have even noticed. Or cared.

What changed?

I was on Facebook sometime in the fall of 2013 and found an old friend. Okay, he was an old boyfriend, but give me credit for being a grown-up and capable having platonic friendships with former lovers. The point is that he knew me pretty well, and he knew that I had always been the type of person who had strong enthusiasms and new interests.

So, he asked me, "What are you passionate about these days?"

Oh, fun! That's one of my favorite questions. Only, I was stumped.

I have never, in decades of life on this planet, *not* had an answer to that question. Usually, I have about twenty-seven or so things that get me jazzed and excited. It bowled me over, as I was sitting there at my computer, to feel a complete blank in response to that question. And it didn't take me long to realize that the big blank blocking me from what I was passionate about was my husband.

We'd been married for thirteen years at that point, and I thought, *Oh my G-d, I don't want to go even another year not feeling passionate about things, or not knowing joy.*

That was another indicator. I think lots of things are fun; I have fun literally every day, even if it's something stupid, like singing to the radio or seeing a pretty bird or whatever. The world is full of wonderful things; we might as well enjoy them, right? Once, I started wondering if other people had fun as much as I do, so I started asking around. I'd say, "When was the last time you had fun?" Again, if it was me, I'd probably tell you something from earlier in the day, or maybe there was a bigger thing, like a trip or a date or something, but I'd have an answer. Lots of my friends had answers too.

Steve, though? I looked at him one day as we were lying in bed and asked, "You know; I was wondering this the other day. When was the last time you had fun?"

He couldn't answer. Nothing. Another big blank. We'd been together over a decade, and he couldn't even pull out a vacation or something with the kids. At that moment, I realized I never wanted to spend time with someone, on any level, in any kind of relationship, who couldn't enjoy their own lives. I don't need to be around thrill seekers, but I want to be around people who actually like being alive and can find fun in the big and the small.

To be honest, most of the real divorce stuff didn't start happening until after my cancer treatment, and it wasn't legally official until October 2016. Really, what happened during this period was that I committed to the *idea* that I wanted a divorce. Steve still lived with us for most of that time (he had a hard time finding his own place), but emotionally it was important for me to know that I didn't have to invest any more energy into a failed relationship.

It sounds horrible (I imagine), but it was easier to say, "I have cancer, and I want a divorce" than, "I have cancer; let's try to make this work." By this point, our marriage was largely formal, anyway, a series of habits and lifestyle entanglements. And the kids, of course. Any attempt to sustain it—and I was the only one likely to make such an attempt—was like throwing love into a black hole.

Not to say he didn't want to save the marriage. He just had a funny way of showing it. For him, it came out more in complaints and criticisms that I would break up the family or kick him out. I started to see how much narcissism made up his personality. Divorce didn't mean losing me or hurting the kids; it meant a black mark on his self-concept and on his image with his friends.

I don't want to wish anyone ill; I didn't want to be one of those people to become even more bitter and to learn to hate her ex during the divorce proceedings. I'm mostly just very sad about it all. There's anger, for sure. I look back and feel a lot of anger that he couldn't be there for me during treatment. That was when I needed my people more than ever, and the one person in the world who should have been there for me complained when I asked him for one thing.

The divorce was finalized over four years ago, so I guess I'm four years wiser. Did I make the right choice? Yeah, I think so. Would I do it again? Um . . .

Maybe?

If I'm being completely honest, raising kids as a single parent truly *sucks*. It is extremely hard—and my kids are pretty independent, and I make good money. It's got to be tough for people in other circumstances. Technically, Steve and I are supposed to be co-parenting, but it shouldn't surprise you by now to know that that isn't going well. He still doesn't have his own place; he's staying with his parents. When the kids visit, they live out of their backpacks. It horrifies me to think about it.

And part of me still wants to help him. He's the father of my children, after all, so if only for their sakes, I'd like to see him stable and somewhat successful. Sometimes I try to nudge him indirectly to do something like take them on an outing, or get them a present they actually want, or take them to a restaurant instead of a drive-through, because I'm so sad that my kids don't have an amazing dad. At this point, I'd settle for a halfway-decent dad. Then I get angry with myself for trying to help, because I've never heard a simple "thank-you" from him, not the slightest show of gratitude. A big blank.

None of this would be any easier, emotionally, with him in the house. But at least someone could get dinner on the way home from work or run a kid to basketball practice or be home with the kids if I have to travel. It's really all about the kids, and I'm all they've got right now. Raising kids takes so much out of you; it's so nice to have someone there with you. Being on your own, knowing that you're the last and only line of defense—it's one of the loneliest feelings you can have.

Yet the fact of the matter is that, even though we lived together the whole time I was going through treatment, I can think of only a handful of times he played a significant role, and at least one of those was a time he pissed me off.

So, no, the cancer didn't change my mind. Single-parenting hasn't changed my mind. But I wouldn't recommend it to anyone either. It sucks. All of it.

15

FiFTY-ONE THiNGS I WANT iN A MAN

1. Is ambitious—in his career, yes, but more importantly, in life.
2. Has a true passion for life and the partner he chose—or else, why bother?
3. Earns enough money to live well—I don't want to be a couple that fights about money all the time because there's never enough.
4. Cares about his health—a basic desire to eat well and take care of his body.
5. Works out—it would be nice if he had a good body too.

My friend Wendy had heard me complaining about Steve for long enough, I guess, because at some point she urged me to make a list of everything I wanted out of a man. This was some time before the cancer diagnosis when I was only beginning to struggle with the idea that my marriage might be failing.

As I've said, I agonized over this question because my vows meant so much to me. Wendy is the kind of person who always has good insights and gives me energy just by being together.

"Make a list," she said. "Think about your ideal man, the things you wanted before you met Steve, or even now, knowing what you know."

"And then what?" I asked. "Give it to Steve like a *Cosmo* quiz?"

"See how many he meets, and then see how important the ones he doesn't are. You may just need to work on smaller things, or maybe there are big things missing that you can't fix. At least you'll know."

6. Is smart—both intellectual and street-smart, someone to go deep with but who can keep his family safe and won't buy the stupid extended warranty.

7. Has a desire to learn—always. I'm always learning and can't stand when my guy seems satisfied with what he already knows.

8. Listens with true interest—because I know the difference between caring about me and just waiting until we can have sex.

9. Is supportive—is it so much to ask for a "Nice work!" or "Congrats!" or "You're a goddess!" once in a while?

10. Acts respectful—I wish this were more obvious to guys.

11. Has pure sexual desire—I've got everything a guy needs, and I expect him to know that and keep his attention where it belongs.

12. Is exciting—maybe even a little scary sometimes, like, in the sense of unpredictable.

13. Finds joy in the children—I didn't expect to love my kids as much as I do, but I do, and my man has to love my kids too.

14. Loves sports—playing them, sometimes; not just watching them.

15. Wants to try things with and without me, but always thinks of me—I want him to have a life of his own and not rely on me for all his socializing, but I also want him to think about whether I'd enjoy something and we can maybe do it together. Or at least let me know he's going to be out with his buddies Thursday night.

16. Wants to kiss all the time—what can I say? I'm an affectionate person.

17. Is not afraid of public affection—see previous.

18. Desires to travel—there's a lot of world to see. It's exciting.

19. Keeps himself clean.

20. Has good hands—is this shallow? I don't know. Not hand-model good, necessarily, but also not covered in calluses or skinny. Good, strong hands that he knows how to use whether in the garage, the yard, the kitchen, or the bedroom.

The process of listing my must-haves in a man felt like putting together a camping checklist. Do I have a canteen? Do I have enough toilet paper? Did I check the canoe for leaks?

Some things I struggled to decide whether they were important enough, like good hands or the PDA. How many pairs of pants do I really need? Will I need heels on this trip? Then there was the question of whether I missed anything. How awful would it be to stake my marriage on a list that didn't include something really crucial to me that somehow was blocked in my brain? Like leaving for the trip and realizing you forgot the tent.

I have no idea why I compared it to camping. I don't actually like camping.

21. *Must dance!*
22. Enjoys live music.
23. Wants to try anything once—though maybe he runs them by me first. Like, no orgies, buddy. I have my lines.
24. Can truly be in love—what do I mean by this? I guess that I'm not just convenient or useful to him; that he takes real pleasure in being with me and doing things with me and for me. And that he can receive love in return; that he's not a big blank or a black hole.
25. Has pure, open communication—just tell me what you're thinking, dammit!
26. Talks and listens—maybe this is repeating #8 and #25. I guess it's important to me.
27. Is capable of making decisions—huh. I don't think twenty-five-year-old Cindy would have put this on her list. This is something I had to learn by being married to a guy who didn't like making his own decisions.
28. Wants to take care of me but doesn't try to do it all the time—I like to feel cared for but not babied.
29. Opens doors for me—a little chivalry goes a long way, guys.
30. *Never* walks in front of me—oops, another lesson from experience.
31. Is not jealous, but attentive.
32. Feels proud to show me off—you don't hide all this at home. Take me out on the town and make the guys jealous!
33. Has my back but confronts me (privately) when I'm wrong—okay, I am wrong once in a while, but I don't need you to throw it in my face in the middle of a party. Damn, that's another "experience" one.
34. Wants to see me succeed.
35. Wants to succeed himself.

The point of the exercise was, hopefully, to remind myself of the important traits Steve had and to help me identify what we really needed to work on. If he was willing to work on those things, then we could make the marriage work. The discouraging thing, though, was how many items I included precisely because Steve *didn't* have them.

36. Is kind to my kids—is this different from #13, "finds joy in my kids"? I'm going to say *yes*. We find joy here and there, but kindness has to happen all the time.
37. Pays on dates—see item #29.
38. Asks me what I want to do, sometimes, and sometimes takes initiative and arranges surprises.
39. Writes me notes and gives me flowers for no reason except he was thinking of me.
40. Tells me I am beautiful without waiting for me to fish for a compliment and without wanting one in return.
41. Excels at his profession—I guess this means he also *has* a profession.
42. Doesn't judge.
43. Has at least one great friend.
44. Is self-confident.
45. Has self-esteem and doesn't need me to constantly build it up, just to be a part of it.
46. Includes me in major decisions; handles the small ones.
47. Is sexually open—I don't know, sometimes I like to try stuff. Let's have some fun and keep things exciting.
48. Acts very social, but respectful.
49. Is romantic.
50. Can cry—at this point I'd settle for any emotional response at all, I think.
51. *Doesn't make assumptions!*—holy crap, I could live a long,

happy life without someone ever again assuming they know what I'm thinking or why I'm doing what I'm doing. Just ask me!

By the time I was done with my list, I knew what was coming. I couldn't even show Steve. What would be the point? It would be like carpet bombing the last vestiges of our relationship, and that was fragile enough as it was. It wasn't even a question of whether Steve could do the work. In the first place, I had no illusions that he would want to. In the second, he'd have to work at almost every item. It didn't feel right to ask him to try to climb Mount Cindy when he lacked the training, the gear, or much of the desire to do so.

My marriage was over. If it had been an actual camping trip, we would have gotten to the site to realize all we had in the car were some old photos and the leftovers from dinner last night. Enough to start making babies with, but good luck lasting the rest of your lives.

While I tell my friends not to get divorced, I do tell them to make lists. They can really clarify things for you and help you order your priorities. No guy will be perfect, and no guy has to be, and I certainly don't want to blast a hole through someone's marriage the way my list did to mine, but sometimes causing acute pain now can prevent years of slow, quiet dying inside.

Good news for you single ladies, though: a good list can really help weed out the schmucks and save you a lot of second and third dates. I've had friends protest that a list would just create unrealistic expectations, but I say we as women have been taught to settle. Too many bad men pass through our lives, and we start to tell ourselves that if he's got one or two redeeming features and is good in bed, it's as much as a girl can ask for.

But check this out: my current boyfriend scores a 50.5 out of 51 on my list! It is possible! The half point off is because he's a tragically bad dancer—but he does dance. And my requirement wasn't *can* dance; it was *must* dance. Shake that booty, baby!

16

THE DUPLEX THEORY

All this divorce stuff is pretty heavy, huh? I'm afraid the only levity I can offer comes from a pretty cynical place, so you may not find it all that funny. Unless you've been divorced. My divorced friends love my marriage advice, but the irony, of course, is that it's too late for them to take it.

Granted, some people have many more divorces under their belts than I do. I am happy to concede that I lack their expertise and have no desire whatsoever to match their achievements. Sometimes I think, *Who am I to give marriage advice?* But if you've never been divorced, then you won't know what it really means unless you hear it from someone who has.

So, when my girlfriends tell me their marriages are rocky and they wonder if they should stay, here's what I tell them: "You don't need a divorce; you need a duplex."

The duplex theory goes like this: It's too hard to parent alone, but you also don't want to go to bed with a husband you can't stand anymore. The solution is to move into a duplex and live next door to one another. He can be around for mowing the yard, chauffeuring the children, and helping clean up after dinner, and at the end of the day, he goes home to his own bed and you go upstairs to yours. You can even put a lock on the door that connects the two units. I guess he can have a lock on his side too.

Look, you can even get a boyfriend. Tell your husband to go get himself a girlfriend. Knock himself out with women. If he can get the oil changed in the car, who cares?

Once the kids are out of the house, or maybe out of college, fine, go get your divorce. You did the hard part and had each other's backs. You deserve a break.

The same goes when my girlfriends meet a great new guy.

"Don't get married, and don't move in together," I say. "Get a duplex."

Even if you didn't like the duplex idea for a married couple with kids, you're going to love this for dating couples. I know; I know. You've fallen in love with the man of your dreams. You're thinking about him all the time. You love being around him and everything about him down to the adorable way he sticks tissues up his nose, twists them, and pulls them out so he can get every last booger this side of the medial turbinate. . . .

I'm sure it's a real cute fest with Mr. Dude there. And immediately you start thinking about getting married and spending your lives together. But why? Do you need the health insurance or something?

Maybe it's the cynical divorced lady in me talking, but how do you know he's the man of your dreams in the first place? Or rather, what makes you so damn sure you're dreaming of the right kind of

guy? We women can be really stupid about what we want in men. All
that stuff that's cute now may not age well. Sure, you think it's sweet
how he tries so hard to fold the clothes but keeps getting wrinkles
in the sleeves of your T-shirts or that he always wants to know what
you're thinking the moment you're ready to fall asleep. But imagine
that ten years down the line, when you're getting kids out the door to
school and you just got out of the shower, and now you need to iron
your T-shirt or go to work with wrinkles. Or you've had a long week,
and all you want to do is sleep, but, dammit, he won't stop talking to
you. You used to think it was great to have no secrets with each other,
but now you think it's okay to poop in private.

Meanwhile, he's thinking that your sixty-two toiletry products,
which used to be like magic vials that you combined to turn yourself
into the dazzling beauty you are, are getting to be a bit too much,
because he's tired of knocking them over every time he reaches for his
toothbrush. Then he says something to you about it, and he's hardly
had time to get his whole complaint out of his mouth when you're
coming right back at him with the way he doesn't put the matching
lids with the Tupperware, and it drives you batshit crazy.

Or, you know, so I imagine it. The point is you really have to have
experience with a good sample size to see all the ways things can go
wrong and to get a good idea of what things look like when they're
going right—and even then, you don't know that they'll stay right.

The good news is that you didn't marry this guy; you just let him
move into the other unit of your duplex. You hang out for meals and
evenings and sex (at least once a day), but you keep your messes on
your own side of the house. Certain occasions are obligatory, like
weddings, funerals, and work parties, and you can still involve him in
some of the household decisions, like replacing the laundry machines
or landscaping the front yard. He can fold wrinkles into his shirts

and have piles of dirty clothes anywhere he wants; you never have to see them. Same for that picture of his mother he likes to keep on the mantel. In this totally fictional example, I'm saying.

The garage is all his. "Go to town, man," you tell him, and he packs it with a bunch of tools he rarely uses and his John Deere riding mower—which he *does* use to mow your lawn. The garden you share as a fun project to do together, though you pick all the flowers and vegetables you planted.

Living apart means you're not on top of each other all the time, which means you can get more excited about seeing each other. Some mornings you unlock your side of the door and sneak into his bed and gently grab his cock—or, as you like to call it, the alarm clock; only it's better than an alarm because now he won't have to masturbate in the shower. You pleasure him; he pleasures you; you orgasm two or three times (may as well enjoy yourself), and then, your favorite part, you retire to your own respective showers. His has a bottle of shampoo and a thumbnail-sized scrap of hand soap; yours has six shampoos and eight conditioners so you can customize your regimen to your mood or the state of the frizz that day. Plenty of room for your three razors (one of which should probably be tossed) and your iPod speaker, and a towel bar for each of your towels, one for your body and one for your hair. There's clearly not enough room for him, anyway, and you never have to hear him complain about how much stuff you need to clean yourself and how the dog can clean herself with just her tongue, so why can't you? Well, listen, buster, if you stopped complaining so much, I could show you what I'd rather use my tongue for that's a lot better than soap.

At night you load the dishwasher—the *right* way—and put away the Tupperware with all the matching lids while he drinks lemonade straight from the container. Hell, he can drink out of the toilet as long as you never have to hear about it. You toss your bra over the shower curtain or the towel rod or onto your bed or anywhere the hell you want to and go to sleep without listening to anyone snore.

"What about the kids?" people like to ask. "What about them?" I say. It's ideal for someone with kids, because you can plop them down in front of a movie or video game on one side while on the other side you guys make out or get work done or totally ignore one another. Your neighbors will want to know how you guys are so relaxed and amiable all the time, and they'll become good friends to try to learn your secrets.

The other day, you were mad at him about some stupid shit or other, and he spent the whole day on his side of the bed, which might as well have been the Netherlands for all you cared. Then when your parents came into town to visit, you let them have your side and skipped the conversation about why you didn't want to give them your bed and sleep on the couch. ("You spent all that money on that couch, Cindy. You'd think it would be comfortable to sleep on." I mean, put your own name in there; I'm just saying . . .) It was fun, at first, because you could pretend you were on a little Airbnb vacation. After a few days together, though, you remembered why you got the duplex in the first place.

If you want to leave, you can. Breaking up could hardly be simpler. He can even keep paying you rent until he mans up and gets his own place. But meanwhile you can get on with your life because almost nothing needs to change. Well, except his installing a deadbolt on his side to keep your crazy ass from busting in some night when you hear grunting noises in the bedroom you used to frequent. Except that, of course.

I know I can say some cynical things, but I really think I've got something with this duplex theory. I bet it could prolong relationships by keeping them fresh and promoting everyone's sanity for what I imagine would be a seven-year term, renewable. It's hard enough to follow through on the responsibilities of any day; why make promises about forever? If you are crazy enough to believe that you can love and cherish the guy for the rest of your life, more power to you, but there's no harm in starting with seven years—in a duplex.

Personally, I will commit to this thing for today, but don't try to pin me down for how I'll feel tomorrow.

17

TONY MAKES ME RADIOACTIVE

FEBRUARY 5, 2014

Oh, Tony, you are the only man on this planet who makes me radioactive!

Not quite the rapturous dialogue of a romance novel, is it? Let me tell you about Tony. Tony, I learned, lives five minutes from my house. He has an eight-year-old daughter who, it turns out, may just know my six-year-old son. You learn a lot when you ask a lot of questions, but this was not a speed dating event. It was an appointment for my PET scan, an imaging procedure that looks at the metabolic activity of cells to help see what's going on in organs and tissues. Tony is the nuclear medicine tech who had the distinct privilege of shooting me up with sodium chloride and radioactive glucose.

To give you an idea of the potency of this chemical soup, it might help to know that they wheel it into the room inside a thick case that looks like it holds top-secret information—or a nuclear weapon. It is so toxic that, as soon as he administers it, Tony leaves the room as fast as he can get me to stop talking so he isn't exposed to his radioactive girl any longer than necessary. Maybe there is material for a romance novel here, or at least a really bad pop song. "Baby, You Light Me Up."

I close my eyes and listen to music for the next ninety minutes while I become fully radioactive. I am glad, now, that no one came with me, as I would feel bad if they went home tonight, only to discover they glow in the dark. The scan is shorter than the CT I had, but the amount of radiation I got in twenty minutes would probably kill a squirrel. Karen would like that little joke. Lori too. (There was this guy; we called him the squirrel. Enough said.)

The PET results process quickly, so I get to look at the scan right away. The radiologist comes in to read the scan and introduces himself as Dr. Poo.

"Excuse me?" I say.

"Dr. Pu. P-U."

"Ohhhh . . ."

He's a sweet man, and I can see he's heard the dumb jokes, so I don't make any, but, *come on*—I'm, like, the poop doctor in my field, and now my doctor's name is . . . That's too good. I can't even say his name without at least smiling.

I look at the film and can see where my pants are hanging around my knees. Just kidding; clothes don't show up on a scan; it just feels very vulnerable. It looks as though there is no bone involvement, meaning the cancer is just in the tissue, but he needs to look more closely. There may be one lesion under my diaphragm. My torso looks like an old lady took her bingo dot marker to my neck and chest. She must have been playing multiple cards. You know the type: they have nine cards going on the table for maximum play, 'cause this way they might win an extra dollar fifty. I'm pretty competitive, so maybe those ladies have something to teach me.

But you get the idea: there are a ton of spots. A scary number

of spots. I know my neck looks thick, and it's not from doing neck
extensions at the gym with 225 pounds on the rack—but I did want
you to know that I can do that. I also have noticed that my left axilla
(armpit) is swollen. All these bingo dots are pushing stuff around
inside, and some things are starting to protrude. I am asymmetrical.

Time for a little Physician's Corner, here. The asymmetry thing is
actually important. None of us is perfectly symmetrical, but most
of us are more or less so. Thus, if you don't already, you should start
looking at yourself in the mirror all the time. I don't mean so that you
can kiss your bicep or so you can admire your long eyelashes. (No, I
don't do that. You do that. Shut up.) No, look so that you learn how
symmetrical you are. When tumors show up in the body, they take up
space, and then you can see a difference in the muscles or soft tissue,
and you can figure something is up. I teach this all the time when
I explain how to properly do a breast exam—and, yes, Tony, this is
for you as well. Start looking! It is important as men can experience
breast cancer too.

Today was about gathering information. Not much changes, really,
except instead of telling people I have four lesions, I can say I light
up like a Christmas tree—or, to my fellow members of the tribe, a
Chanukah bush.

On the way home, I stopped to see one of my *Winning!* teammates,

Kristin. Not only is she an awesome gift, but she also gave me an awesome gift. The visit started with a hug and ended with a bottle of the patchouli and orange body spray that she makes with such love. Patchouli is my favorite oil and scent, and it is timely. With all the enzymes and vitamins, I am detoxing, and sometimes I can smell the chemicals seeping out of me. Gross, I know, but it's part of the program. I hope this time around I don't dump it all over my SUV. The body spray, not my chemicals. It did smell good in there for a few months, though.

Lisa, my sister, texted me that afternoon to see how my scan went. I replied with honesty and humor, 'cause that's how I roll. Actually, the last time I rolled was at the Bears' game down a hill with the kids before we went to the parking lot, but I digress. She said, and I quote, "I am awed by your courage and attitude." Had she stopped there, that would have been fabulous. However, she then proceeded to tell me I could let my guard down, because she could handle whatever I had to bring.

"No, really, I'm good," I replied.

"I want you to feel comfortable being afraid or tired or whatever," she wrote back. "It's okay."

Except that I really felt fine, so I told her again. She finally let it drop. Why is it so hard to believe that someone can be great through this diagnosis and experience? Stay awed, world, because I am not changing a thing.

It was a busy day. I also stopped at the Cancer Center in Mokena to see what goes on there. Free wigs, turns out. How cool is that?

"You can pick one new one or as many as you want from the 'used' bin," explained the nice lady behind the counter.

Oy, I don't want to seem ungrateful, but I'm going to go with new. Jamie, a volunteer, was there to help me find the right one. She pulled out a bunch of options, and I picked what I wanted. I wish I could get a pair of cowboy boots to go with the wig. Something about it says, "Howdy, pardner."

That's another item off my Winning Against Cancer checklist. Then there is the question of yoga—not happening unless I let Kristin, also a yoga instructor, torture me. Art classes and journaling—maybe. Kids' Club program—ran that past the kids, and they said they might try a few classes. Cool. I can do this.

Coincidentally, the Cancer Center has a sister center in Homewood, where I have lectured about the benefits of acupuncture quite a few times. It is also dedicated to Dr. Ritchie Desser, a great family friend who passed from cancer many years ago. Six degrees of separation even in illness . . . or in this case, only two.

Well, it's after ten o'clock, and I am choosing to go to sleep. Tonight, I am next to my son Ari, who could not look more peaceful as he sleeps. He does that perfectly. I will try to emulate him. Sweet dreams.

18

Hope is a Choice

"Hope, *v. To want something to happen or be true."*
—*Merriam-Webster.com Dictionary*

A great friend once shared with me that she dislikes the word *hope*. She finds it too passive. For example, when we say to someone, "I hope you have a great day," we're expressing a desire for something to happen to them over which none of us has any control. Compare that with "Make it a great day!" That is a call to action.

I really like that, and I have become more aware of when and how I use the word *hope*—especially during treatment. When we receive a diagnosis, we hope we will get better, hope there is a cure, hope there is an answer, and hope we can get through it. That sounds so hopeless, though, like it's all in someone else's hands. We should say, "Make it better," "Make a cure," "Make an answer," and "Make it through." Those sound so much more inspiring and as though there is no other choice.

Choice is interesting to me too. It disturbs me when people say, "I had no choice." Like, *no* choice, at all? That seems unlikely. I believe we always have a choice. We may not like some of the options or the outcomes, but there is always a choice. I choose to be happy; I choose to have fun every day, and I chose to beat cancer. I am; I do; and I did. I could have chosen differently, but I didn't, and I am satisfied with and even grateful for my decisions.

On the flip side of this are the people who think they have control over other people's choices and feelings. You should do this. You should feel that. You can do better. You are wrong. I think you have a choice in how you feel about your life, but I don't believe I can make you feel that way. Maybe that's too subtle a difference.

I hope that people will wake up and stop doing this. See what's wrong with that statement? It is filled with a desire that I have no control over. *I make my life fabulous, and I learn from my decisions, and I allow myself to feel emotions so that I may grow personally from them.* So much more empowering. I feel better just writing it.

I don't want to give anyone hope. I want to be supportive and caring. I want to exude strength and fortitude and intelligence and joy.

I walk down the street, and people notice me. I constantly meet people who want to be around me. I have trouble finding people whom I want to spend time with because most are full of hope instead of action. There is a perfume called Success, and I wear it. Took me a lot of years to discover my scent, but I am perfecting it and pouring it on.

I watched a father tell his very young daughter to stay away from another kid and a parent in the pool. I was down in Hollywood, Florida, on a little vacation, doing a lot of resting by the pool. The divorce lawyer said not to travel by myself, that it could hurt my custody case, so I took the kids with me. (Turns out a bad lawyer also hurts your case.) So, this man says to his daughter, "You have been bothering them for an hour, and it is enough. I know what it's like to be with you for an hour and how hard that is."

He actually said that. To his own child. I almost spoke up, but since they passed the concealed carry laws, I am careful what I say, and besides, it was none of my business. What I did do was get sad for a moment for that young girl and the messages she must get. We all make choices, and her father made one that I believe to be very harmful. Maybe she'll thrive in spite of his comments. Even though the exchange I witnessed was not mine to fix, I wish I had said something kind or encouraging to her. Maybe it would have dampened the negative delivery her father used.

A wish, like hope, is hobbled by inaction.

I don't believe that we are designed to be alone. I truly enjoy hours, if not days, by myself, but even then, there is still interaction with people. Even if I travel by myself, there are still flight attendants and waiters and hotel clerks. True solitude I have never tried. I think I will never marry again—I probably shouldn't have in the first place. I don't think most people should marry, though I don't know why anyone should listen to me.

At any rate, I hope for nothing. I need to be able to take action, like manifesting. Instead of hoping, I will attempt to choose a good man and make the best of my relationships, and I will bring love to me in my life.

19

Not Great

MARCH 20, 2014

So much to catch up on. I have just been cruising along. I think that is really easy to do when you don't have to face treatment quite yet. I am learning a lot about myself. I am strong, determined, brave, creative, and positive. Those things I knew, but they've been tested in new ways, and I'm grateful to find them confirmed. I am struggling to admit, however, that I am tired and occasionally unable to do everything I want to. That is new.

I had a great conversation with Spencer last week. Here is how it went:

Spencer: How are you today?

Cindy: Fantastic!

Well, that is how our conversations usually start. My normal answer, every time, is, "Fantastic!" This time, however . . .

Cindy: I haven't decided yet, today. I will make a decision later. . . . OMG, did that really come out of my mouth?

This all leads to me saying: Honestly, I am having a hard time. I am tired, for me, and I am anxious about treatment.

Yada, yada, yada.

Knowing Spencer like I do, I knew there was not going to be any typical "Rah-rah, go get 'em!" speech, for which I was truly thankful. The Gipper can bite me. Instead, he asked me why I said the words *honestly* or *to be honest* before I answered. He proceeded to tell me that I am one of the most trustworthy people he knows and that I don't need to insist on being honest because I *am* honest. Not to mention, sometimes people say that when they are lying and trying to convince you they are being truthful.

Hmm . . . that gets me thinking, and then I figure it out. I am not trying to tell Spencer that I am honest. I am trying to convince myself that it is okay to admit that I am struggling with a few things, which makes me vulnerable. I was thinking that a confession like this makes me weak, and I was trying to justify admitting to that.

But there is a *humongous* difference between being weak and being vulnerable. Weakness, the inability to rise to the occasion, is not a great attribute. Vulnerability, however—wow, this is where we learn who we are, where we are, and how much we can grow as a result. We open ourselves up to the most amazing possibilities in personal growth when we accept vulnerability as an asset. Because I could admit to feeling tired and anxious, I diminished some of the power those emotions have over me and found emotional support in a good friend.

I am now fantastic!

Everyone should have a Spencer in their lives. However, you first need to be in a place to receive gifts of knowledge and to improve oneself. If you are not ready, well, then . . . a friend like Spencer will go underappreciated and will likely be misinterpreted. Incidentally, if you *are* ready, I am not open to sharing him. Go find your own damn Spencer.

I got vitamin C on Tuesday. This is my third time. It makes me cold and dehydrated, so I need lots of water, a stick of lip balm, and comfy blankets, and everything is good.

"Getting vitamin C" means either going to the clinic or sitting in a comfy chair at home and hooking up an IV bag of vitamin C. Then the nurse, my soon to be ex, or my kid will stick the IV into the bouncy ball in my chest or into my inner elbow. Now we can turn on the drip and let the yummy nutrients into my body. Vitamin C is an antioxidant, so the idea here is to set it loose against all the free radicals produced in my blood from all the stress of treatment.

Yesterday was my first chemo treatment. Lori picked me up, and I started crying. Team Winning! What happened to the girl who was proclaiming her favorite day was the day she was diagnosed with cancer? In fact, the tears—or the emotions behind them—were a continuation of the day before. So much negativity. Gotta get rid of that. It is equivalent to poison for the mind, and I'm already getting poison in my body.

My soon-to-be ex did *not* follow up on a commitment to pick up my dry ice for my Penguin caps (the cooling head coverings that can help reduce chemo-induced hair loss), and I allowed that to increase my stress level. My sister kept me company during the vitamin C treatment, and after one perceived negative comment, I told her if I heard one additional one, she would have to leave. I don't want a glass that is always 85 percent empty. I think I may start to rate people on a scale of how full or how empty their glass is. There will be a minimum requirement of fullness if you're going to be around me, say 65 percent.

Then my mother texted, and instead of telling me how great I would do with the Penguin caps, she was all on about how if they were horrible, at least I would have tried. Don't ever hire her to do the halftime speech for a losing team. I rate her text 70 percent empty. *Ugh*. Neither of them meant to be negative, but perception is everything. Maybe I just needed a challenge today.

But I was talking about yesterday morning and my first chemo treatment. Lori was starting to cheer me up, when here comes Spencer's call. He starts with, "I was thinking: If I ever had to go through what you have to, what would I think about? The first thing I thought was I would have a picture of the Incredible Hulk, only I would get a friend to draw my face on him. I would hang it on the wall where I could see it and enter beast mode to attack this thing."

I decided that I would not look as good as the Incredible Hulk. Too big and too green. Same goes for She-Hulk, though she's at least got the body. I am going with Wonder Woman, as I have the boobs for the outfit. Between Lori and Spencer, I finally get in the mood I should have been in all along.

We arrive an hour late for treatment. Traffic and rain. We live in Chicago. How is it that rain freaks everyone out, and they forget how to drive? Lindsey is my nurse. We know each other from somewhere but can't figure out where. We went to the same college, but she is much younger than I am. She worked at RUSH, where I had Reese. She worked in HEME with Dr. Henry Fung, who was my mother's hematologist. But it doesn't seem like any of those. We will keep trying until we figure it out; it's the kind of problem you want to focus on while someone's stabbing your bouncy ball with an IV needle.

First step: IV nutrients, including B vitamins, glutathione (an antioxidant), etc. Then Rituxan because I tested CD20 positive. That means there's a certain antigen on the cancerous white blood cells, and Rituxan is like a man-made antibody that goes after cancer cells with CD20 (believe me, this is the layman's version). Then I got some premeds, which included Benadryl. That was probably what caused the paresthesia (prickly, tingling sensation) in my legs and toes. Started to feel totally sleepy, and my speech slowed. Wish I could remember if I said anything stupid or hilarious. The Rituxan gave me a sore throat and bad ear pain like when a plane is taking off. That lasted thirty minutes after they gave me more meds to combat it.

Then, at last, the chemo, ABVD.

I was given more drugs yesterday than I think I have had in thirty years. But, okay. I will become one with the drugs and heal. Didn't Darth Vader say something like that, or am I still hallucinating from the pharmaceuticals?

Forty minutes before chemo, I started the Penguin cold caps. I would not lose my hair on my head; that was decided. I was excited to lose hair on my vulva, though, as Brazilians were costing me $80 a pop. The cold caps were $580 a month to rent, $60 for coolers to transport, and $180 in dry ice each session. By comparison, I suppose the Brazilian sounded like a deal; frankly, it felt better than the cold cap too.

The caps must be kept at −32°F. The first cap gave me a headache that would be equal to if not worse than sticking ice-cold pokers in my eyes. That lasted about ten minutes. We changed the caps several times an hour during the active part of the treatment. The headaches lessened with each one, and by the fourth or fifth, they were gone, probably because at that point, I was thoroughly frozen. I once sat through an entire Bears game at night in −8° weather, so I thought, *Well, that's just a wee bit colder and on my head. I can handle that, right?* I think the whiskey helped at the Bears game, though. I told the nurse next time I wanted whiskey in my port, and she agreed—as long as I was sharing.

Dr. Udrian, my oncologist, visited with me and talked about Neulasta. It's meant to stimulate the production of white blood cells to replace those killed during chemo, but it can have some nasty side effects, like kidney problems and capillary leak syndrome. Not sure what to do there. I wanted to trust Dr. Udrian. He was great; he hugged everyone. What oncologist does that? Dr. Udrian and Lindsey definitely rated as a cup 85 percent full or higher. They were keepers. I liked the new additions to my team. Winning!

Lori sat with me all day. Not a complaint. Love her. She helped me change the caps. We got a great picture of me wearing one and smiling like I was being paid to model them. If they were made of brown leather, they would look like I was ready to play football back in the olden days. They were blue, however, which I didn't love. I wished they were orange or red; I think I would have liked the way they looked better. Or at least dark blue and orange, 'cause then I could wear them to Bears games.

Treatment took about eight hours. You have to wear the caps not just during treatment but for five hours after that, so I was up until 11:00 p.m. changing caps. At that point, Lori had to go home, so I got my boys involved. Ari helped me change a few of them, while Jackson pulled my hair to see if I could feel it. You've got to love their different approaches to this. Ari will make a great boyfriend someday. Jury is still out on Jackson, but he sure is funny.

Lori and Spencer are my rocks. Between the two of them, I know I have support where I want it. If you don't have friends like that, then start asking the universe to provide them. Better yet, be that kind of friend to someone else, and you will see the payback increased tenfold.

Okay, so maybe I'm not fantastic right now, but I do have a lot to be grateful for. Like friends and my family who don't freak out when I'm not Wonder Woman all the time.

But I'm still Wonder Woman most of the time.

20

I Decide What Hair I Lose

Can I confess something? One of my first thoughts after diagnosing myself was that I *did not* want to lose my hair. Is that vain? Okay, maybe I'm vain.

Or maybe it's just one of those human thoughts you have when you don't know what to think. You don't know what you're going to think until you actually have to think something in that moment. I thought about my kids and my career, my parents, and my friends too.

But I definitely thought about my hair. In fact, the first time I cried, it was over my hair. An oncology nurse told me that around week three of chemo, I would wake up and find all my hair on my pillow. Something about that image felt more real than so much else of what was happening, and the tears came all on their own.

I guess I had to get something out of my system, because after that, I grew determined. I said to myself, *I will not lose my hair. I just won't.* As if by willing, I could make it so. There are things we can will into the world; I really believe that. But other things are just science.

When my friend Mike insisted I seek allopathic care, I knew I was facing almost certain chemical baldness.

Like I do with any challenge, though, I sprang into action. Once I accepted the fact that I was facing down the loss of my hair, I contacted my friend Melinda, who is a professional photographer.

"You've got to help me," I told her. "I've needed a new headshot for forever, and now I'm about to lose my hair. Please find some time for me to come get new shots of me now before I look different."

"Absolutely!" she said. Welcome to the team, Melinda.

The funny thing is that I never really identified much with my hair. Even as a kid. I had that bad, frizzy, Jewish hair that you can't do anything with. Think Gilda Radner, who I used to think was my long-lost sister. If anything, I should have been happy to see it go. Roll the dice and see if I don't get better hair afterward. I've had patients who were very matter-of-fact about it and preemptively shaved their heads, but I couldn't imagine that.

You want to know what it really was? It was the fear of people—like, my friends, but also random people on the street—looking at me and thinking, *Oh, she must have cancer.* That's what I really didn't want. To be sick or to be thought of as sick with cancer.

Melinda is actually the wife of my friend Bob, who owns the gym where I used to train. She was more of an acquaintance, but I'd seen her work and loved it—much more creative than the conventional stuff of holding hands and flowers, much more about the drama and energy of the moment. Beyond that, I felt a real connection to her. How much more reason did I need?

"Make sure to schedule your makeup for beforehand," she told me. Ha. I don't really do makeup. Even when I've done video work, there's Greg, who sprays my hair and maybe uses some powder, but I don't have him do any makeup. I may put on some eyeliner if you're lucky—but don't count on getting lucky, buddy. Unless I'm wearing mascara. Then you know I'm in a bit of a wild mood.

Melinda knew a makeup artist who could help. So, I go to see this woman, and she's lovely and kind and very professional, and she puts me over the top. The whole nine yards: eyeliner, eyeshadow, lipstick, blush, powder—oh, and that stuff that goes on before all the other stuff.

I know what it's called, but I kind of wish I didn't.

And, look, I'm sure she knew what she was doing, but when she finished, I looked in the mirror and didn't recognize myself. Perhaps if I'd been more in the habit of using makeup, I would have appreciated what she'd done with me. As it was, I could see I looked beautiful, but I didn't look like me. I left for Melinda's, feeling like I had some theatrical mask on. I wondered if any of my friends would even recognize me if they saw me right then.

We arrived at Melinda's studio, a neat little space in her basement. *We* comprised me, Ari, and Jackson, who came with me partly out of curiosity and partly out of boredom.

"Let's get some shots with the boys," Melinda said, so we did a bunch of shots with me standing or sitting next to or between my boys. They weren't really dressed for the occasion, and I don't know that they liked the attention, but I thought it was sweet. It's a mother's prerogative to get her children to pose with her once in a while, especially when she has cancer.

Some of my friends wanted to go wig shopping with me. Laura was the one who actually did. She and I became friends leading our kids' Girl Scout troop, which was more like arts and crafts with a big party rather than a lesson to earn a new badge. That sounds like exactly the kind of thing I would do. Go out with the ladies, have some fun with it. I joked to Melinda that I should host a wig party. Some of my friends have purse and buckle parties; some have cooking parties; some have sex toy parties, which are certainly entertaining, but I think I would be the first in my group of friends to have a wig party. As soon as I mentioned this as chitchat during our photo session, Melinda said she would bring a backdrop and take pictures. Add a little wine, and we've got ourselves a party! The idea of a wig party photo shoot was way more exciting to me than the session for my headshot. There is something that just screams fun about a bunch of tipsy ladies posing in hair that once belonged to someone else.

I try to look at my life as a series of tiny opportunities to have fun, to learn, to better myself, and, quite honestly, to impact others around me in a positive way. The headshot would be good for my website; the wig party photo shoot would be good for our souls. It would create a moment in time for laughing and smiling and maybe crying that we would remember for years. Jackson offered his multicolored Mohawk he won at a carnival. I thought that could be my first picture, and it would be the funniest until I got one with a cold cap on.

Then it was time to get a few headshots. I've done this a couple times before, and each time I think I could never be a model. The instructions always confuse me right away. Tip your chin up. Now turn your ear down. Turn a little to your right, but look left. Okay, now tip your shoulders to the left and your hips to the right while your head does a sort of circle à la *The Exorcist*.

The first time I put on the Penguin cold cap, it felt like someone stuck

a thousand ice picks into my head. It felt like that for twenty minutes.
How much was this costing me? $7,000? Out of pocket? And I had
to do this every time I got chemo for the next six months? Awesome.
I must have been nuts. And vain, remember, and possibly wasting my
time.

I'm so all in.

I had to tell my oncologist about the cold cap because so few
people use them. Basically, it's a supercold wrap that goes around
your head and causes your follicles to hibernate so they don't absorb
the chemicals and die. To keep them cold, you have to store them
in a cooler full of dry ice or a deep freezer and handle them with
special gloves. To protect your scalp, you make this moleskin cap
that goes over your forehead and ears. You don't want to get frostbite
for anything less than climbing a mountain in Nepal, which I would
totally do if I could get a Sherpa to carry me. Or a helicopter. I like
a little hiking, but days in the elements just to get somewhere, turn
around, and spend days getting back down again? That sounds like
something people do when they don't have things like cancer to teach
them life lessons.

It's not just one cap either. It's several that you have to put on in
a series. You put on the first one for forty minutes before you start a
session of chemo, change to the second and third one every twenty
minutes, and then keep changing them every forty minutes for the
next seven hours. Yes, I said *seven hours.*

Lori was usually my companion for chemo, and she was a
superstar. You weren't supposed to allow more than two minutes
between caps, which meant you had to have your shit together. We'd
set a timer, and at a specific moment before the one had to come off,
Lori would go to the freezer for the next one. I'd be loosening the
straps while she brought the new one over and would help me get
it on and tighten the straps up. After three or four weeks, we had it

down to a science. It was kind of fun, actually, being that in tune with one another, like relay runners perfectly passing the baton. It was a challenge we could overcome. We're both pretty competitive like that.

As I've tried to describe, the cold caps caused the most excruciating pain I've ever felt—including my pregnancies and having kidney stones. I'd take migraines over those any day. Picture the worst brain freeze you've ever had, then spread it all over your skull at about one hundred times the intensity. Or the ice picks, wielded by spiteful leprechauns who got kicked out of Ireland.

Thankfully, the worst of it is over after the first twenty minutes. When you first put one on, the discrepancy between the cap, which is at −32°F, and your scalp is huge, and what you're feeling is the blood vessels constricting really quickly. By the time we had to swap out that first one, my head was cold enough to keep vegetables frozen, so I would be more or less acclimated and really couldn't tell the difference when the new one went on.

And all to keep hair that I never really liked anyway. Or rather, all to not be thought of as sick. The irony, of course—and there had to be irony in a situation like this—was that everyone who saw me on our drive home with this big blue wrap around my head must certainly have thought I was sick—or just let out of a sanitarium. I didn't even try to hide it, really. How could I? Lori and I would wave at people when they gawked, big goofy smiles on our faces. Once we stuck our heads out the window and screamed just to, you know, lean in, I guess. You want to talk about irony: there was even a time I wore them to get my Brazilian wax.

Since my time, they've come out with a new product, the DigniCap, which looks like an old-fashioned canister vacuum. You still have a cap, but the unit pumps the cold air in, so there's less of the hassle of swapping the old ones out. It is covered by insurance now, for those going through breast cancer. Guess Hodgkin's isn't important or popular enough for the insurance companies.

You know what, though? I'd do it all again. In a heartbeat. It felt that important to me, and since then, I've been able to share my experience with so many women so they can do the same if it's important to them.

Melinda wrapped up and I offered to pay her, but she absolutely refused. Part of me thinks that was sweet and part of me wishes I could give her what she's worth for her time. It's that weird place cancer puts you in. You know people want to help, and you want to let them, but you also don't want to feel like you're the helpless sick person. At least, I didn't.

The most unexpected part of the whole hair thing was how my hair changed. Most women don't like how their hair comes back, and I definitely wasn't happy when I started noticing the early changes. It began to thin, and you could see some gray growing out, and the curl was different. Eventually, I got used to it, and now I rather like it. There's less frizz and more of a wavy curl happening; I feel like I can do something with it now.

I don't care for the gray, though. I used to be brown with reddish highlights, which I did like. When I went gray, I decided to try going blonde. They warn you about doing anything to your hair while you're using the caps—no dye, no product, no heat—so my stylist was really cautious when I said I was ready to try something with it. She wound up just dying a patch and sending me home to see what happened.

She was right too. Can you imagine if I'd spent all that time, money, and energy to keep my hair only to lose it afterward because I was impatient for it to have some color? Like I need more irony in this situation.

Pubic hair is another story. It's still very important to me, but for the opposite reason. Every six weeks, I pay eighty dollars to have Tracy slather my labia majora and minora with hot wax in order to rip all the hair off at lightning speed. Then it's a race to see if I can grab my poor, stinging skin before she starts in again. A race to the bald labia. Tracy would laugh while I lay there in tears. Isn't it supposed to be pleasurable when someone touches your labia?

The hot wax gets intimate with not only the outside of my vagina but the crease in my crotch, the inner lips, and my butt crack. The upside is I naturally do not have hair on my butt hole, which I have learned from Tracy can sometimes be excessive. Again, I pay for this hair removal. Rumor has it others pay for it too. Are we insane? Is it worth it? At least we know we can get everything clean when we poop.

Let's discuss how waxing can, in fact, be of enormous benefit. First, it is about cleanliness. I have to tell you: I have done a lot of Pap smears, and toilet paper does not get stuck on bald labia. Fuzz from your new pajamas does not need to be handpicked off your private area when you have no hair there. But let's be honest. Cleanliness is always a bonus, but the biggest benefit comes on opening day at the pool. Ladies, you all can relate to that experience of lying on the chair at the side of the pool thinking, *I worked really hard for this bikini body this year*, and feeling all sexy. You are on your back, legs slightly apart so you can gently flex your quads because you've been to the gym all winter and you want people to notice that teardrop that pops out when you flex. Toes are gorgeous because you just got a pedicure, and there is hot pink polish on them so they pop with a tan. The bikini is new, and you are so excited about how hot you look in it.

Okay, even if you slept through your pedicure appointment because you were too drunk last night, you think your suit would look better on your grandma, and you wish the kids would stop splashing you with water, the actual realization that you are about to have is the same.

You sit up, cross your legs Indian style (I know that's not politically correct, but tough. I am old enough that it was called that when I went to school, and "crisscross applesauce" is just stupid and certainly not what is happening in this situation, as will become apparent). Suddenly, there it is . . . a single pubic hair, possibly the longest pubic hair anyone has ever grown, poking its way out from the hem of your suit like it's looking for food. Yes, you missed a pubic hair when you were shaving, and you just know that everyone at the pool has *not* missed it but noticed it long ago and has been talking about you this whole time. And now it's waving hello to all the world, like it wants them all to look down at your groin, and if they weren't looking before, they surely are now, if for no other reason than that you just looked at it and yelped and are still staring at it like you just discovered this groin belonged to somebody else and you misplaced your own (if only). And there is nothing you can do about it, because you do not have the superhuman grip it takes to pinch this wayward follicle between finger and thumb and yank it out without it slipping through your grasp. But you try anyway, desperate to remain inconspicuous while you grab it and pull on it, like, twenty times. And now you're in tears, but it still hasn't budged, so you figure the next best thing is to conceal it. You try to tuck it back in under the suit, but besides being the longest and friendliest pubic hair in the world, it is the coarsest son of a bitch and straight as a lightsaber, and it will poke through your suit rather than obediently lie flat. For the rest of the day, then, you walk around with a towel wrapped around your waist, begging the kids to go home because you have never wanted so badly to shave your crotch.

When you finally get home, you're irritated about the ridiculous tan lines from the towel. You hop directly in the shower to shave that nasty little hair so that you don't get distracted by the kids trying to roast marshmallows at the stove or something. That's when you see five or six more of the little buggers. How can the lighting in your shower really be better than the sun that lights up the entire friggin' planet? And now you're just grateful you won't have to show off your bikini body again that day. If you hadn't worked so hard to get in shape, maybe you would have worn one of those tennis-dress bathing suits and avoided all this drama, but you really like that bikini. . . .

And that is why I pay to have this vagina waxed bald, truly bald. I think it feels great, too, in addition to avoiding the pool-day mortifications. A soft, smooth vagina is so nice compared to one with crazy, curly, Gilda Radner hair all over the place.

Of course, there's always the question of what to do in between appointments with Tracy. The hair begins to grow back, reclaiming its lost territory. If I shave, I am left with those tiny little bumps on my skin, which are not as fun to touch. So, what are my options? Let the woolly mammoth return until my monthly rendezvous with the hot wax jar? My mind doesn't like forced choices, so I start getting creative.

For instance, my son plays football. I am a crazy-excited sideline mom, always cheering for him till I'm hoarse. Occasionally, he cuts a lightning bolt or his team number on the side of his head or on the side of his Mohawk. . . . You see where this is going. Yes! Why not? What if I had a lightning bolt or a heart or, I don't know, Zac Efron's name carved out of my vulva hair? (Call me, Zac!) It's not like anyone would have to know (except me and Zac). Except, knowing me, I might feel compelled to start a naked pool-party club to show it off. Is there a secret section on Facebook where you can post your pubic art pictures? I could call Melinda and throw another party. Pubic hair art party with photo booth. Another first among my friends.

What else could I do? Braiding with beads! Coloring with streaks of hair chalk! Oh my goodness, the possibilities are endless. Where would this end? Send ideas, dear reader. We'll make a coffee-table book. One that people would actually read, I bet. I have another idea for a book, too, called *My Douche Bag Is Bigger Than Your Douche Bag: An Anthology of Exes*. Anyone with an ex will feel solidarity in hearing others' horrible stories, and we'll give out copies to our friends who don't believe us when we tell those stories and say, "See; it's not just me. Ex-husbands are the worst!"

Chemo didn't help here, incidentally. With the pubic hair. Those annoying little hairs just hung on and laughed at me for freezing my scalp every week to keep the hair I actually wanted. Cancer offers so few opportunities to find the positive that you grasp at straws over little conveniences like losing hair or weight, even if you know it's for bad reasons. But I didn't even get the little straws. Oh well, I had it easier than most in other ways.

Vain or not, I can't help but think of how my hair communicates to the world, and I'd like to be as in control of the message as possible. It's something I took for granted most of my life until I was faced with the possibility of having it taken from me. Then it suddenly felt like one of the most important things to me, frizz notwithstanding. I'd take frizzy any day over bald. On my head anyway.

When I pulled Melinda's photos from the envelope for the
first time, I scowled a little. Not because they were bad. They were
amazing, beautiful. But I didn't recognize myself. Cindy Howard, DC,
DABCI, DACBN, FIAMA, FICC, glamorous professional. No, sorry. It
just wasn't working for me; it wasn't the way I saw myself or wanted
to see myself in my mind.

Months later, when my hair turned gray and the frizz eased up,
they looked even less like me. I look back on the whole experience,
and I'm still glad I did it. It was fun, and Melinda does great work.
But those pictures show a woman trying to hang onto something that
no longer exists, not the woman who fought to give herself a future
that hasn't been written.

I look like what I look like. The rest doesn't matter anymore.

21

SHE SAID A LOT OF PEOPLE DON'T LIKE ME

MARCH 31, 2014

Today I was told a lot of people don't like me. They are jealous of me.
How ridiculous is that?

What is there to be jealous of? My mother is terminal; I've got
this failed marriage that won't seem to go away; I still miss my dead
dog, Gunnar; and, oh, I have cancer.

My psychic asked me how I was doing, and I told her I felt
ridiculously great. Everyone with cancer should feel as great as I do.
Everyone with cancer should have the attitude I do. Everyone with
cancer should be as grateful as I am. Everyone without cancer should
have these blessings too.

Not fifteen minutes later, she's telling me there are a lot of people
pretending to like me but secretly not liking me. I couldn't help
wondering if she was talking about herself. I suppose I shouldn't go

around saying I feel great even though I'm doing chemotherapy, but it's true, so what am I supposed to say?

"Cindy"—sympathetic head cock—"how are you doing?"

"Oh, you know. . . ."

"Well, you look great."

"Oh, thanks, you're sweet. I mean, I usually do, because I train hard and I eat great, so . . ."

"I'm sorry, I didn't mean—"

"That I don't normally look great, or that I look great for a sick person? 'Cause I'm sorry to disappoint you, but I feel as great as I look."

Yeah, okay, so as you can see, I don't think trying to play to people's expectations would go well for me. I can only say what's true.

The psychic also told me that my heart is affected. That's the third time my heart has come up in a few weeks. No surprise, I guess, given my marriage. But July and August are my months for opportunity. Until then, I am to sit still.

She sees no death in the next three months. In fact, she says I have a long life line. One hundred twelve, here I come.

She says Steve was "influenced" by a woman three years ago. Okay . . . Do I care about this or not? I don't like not knowing things and being lied to, but at this point, what difference does it make? I will sign the papers in six weeks.

She says it's okay to sign them but to be careful.

My heart has been broken, and I am not ready to be hurt again.

I am very driven, she says. No kidding.

Steve and I will never be friends. That one's a little harder. After all the history, and with our kids, I'd like to at least be on good terms. But she says he is selfish and has taken me for granted. Yep, can't argue there.

I have two close friends whom I shouldn't trust; they are jealous of me. That's never good to hear.

I need to heal my spirit. Huh.

I have a guide who sits on my right side, especially in my car. Someone who passed over eight years ago. He is male. I have no idea who this could be.

She doesn't see me as sick. That's interesting, because neither do I. Did I tell her that yet?

I will be fine financially.

I will be successful in business. That part is already true.

My aura is yellow and green, indicating leadership and healing resonance. No real surprises there. I guess the big takeaway is that some people in my life are not being straightforward with me. Under other circumstances, I might be able to care more. As things stand, I'm sure it's not Lori, Kristin, or Wendy, and that's good enough for now.

I started with Laurie Grice, a naprapath, last Monday. The first appointment was for connective tissue work.

She did her thing on me, then told me, "You're so driven, you could give some of your drive away to twelve other people and still have more than enough for yourself. But you're on sympathetic overload. Your heart is broken."

My heart, again. But I feel great, don't I? Yes. And no. I need to fix that.

Two and a half weeks ago, I started reiki again with Kathy. She uses a lot of imaginative work to help my body relax and heal itself.

"Go somewhere you feel healthy," she said.

"The beach," I told her. "I'd like to stick my feet in the sand."

Strangely, though my head said *beach*, my body put me in a rain forest, standing on rocks with water rushing through my legs. Rain was pouring down around me, but immediately above me, the sun was shining.

Consciousness and spirit expert Caroline Myss says when AIDS, which is an immune disorder, became a big deal, we were also beginning to destroy the rain forests. Then my mind sent me to the rain forest to heal my immune system. Makes sense.

Kathy saw a lotus flower on my heart. Kept going to my heart chakra. She says I give too much with my heart, but I don't receive enough in return. That should be my focus: receiving. That one's going to be hard for me.

During our second reiki session, I couldn't get out of my head or ground my feet. I experienced a lot of migratory pain.

Kathy saw a gondola with someone in it, and in fact I've been casually considering a trip to Italy. Doesn't someone have to steer the gondola?

What's that? What about my cancer? You mean my time capsules? I didn't take the Neulasta for immunity, which has pitted my doctors against one another. Dr. Udrian says it's okay; Dr. Block wants me on it. Here is my deal: no Neulasta. Too many side effects. Next question.

I ran a complete blood count to check my neutrophils. Those are your most numerous white blood cells. Thus, if they are low, I am in trouble; high is good.

They were high: eighty-eight.

I've been taking echinacea and elderberry to raise my neutrophils. Guess it's working. No eggs or raw nuts either. Got through this two-week cycle, awesome.

Will negotiate the Neulasta next time.

Today is Day Twelve. I think a little of my hair came out—very little, so it could be paranoia. Got to get through ten more days. I will. I have been wearing my hair curly since I cannot use heat during treatments if I want to keep it. I think it looks crazy, but people seem to like it. So many say I am cute and that I look younger. That is a good thing, I suppose.

I taught in Saint Louis last weekend at the DABCI getaway (a chiropractic internist thing). My friend Larry from Professional Health Products knows about my time capsules. He is sending me a mushroom complex and enzymes. He wanted to know if I would still spit cherries with him. That is a good story for another time. I said yes as long as they are Bing cherries. Maraschino cherries are so unhealthy.

So many people want to help me.

Virginia hooked me up with vitamin C IVs to do at home and wouldn't charge me for the first month of supplies. She told my friend Delilah that she can't handle that I am sick. I assured her that I am not sick and that I will be back next year to lecture. But I understand her concern: Jack, her husband and one of my mentors, died two years ago of cancer.

My friend Sara set up a schedule for people to cook and bring me dinner three days a week. I didn't want people to go out of their way for something I was still capable of doing (because I'm Wonder Woman, dammit!), but now that I've had a few of these wonderful offerings, I don't ever want them to stop. Great gluten-free, dairy-free, sugar-free meals. New things I don't make. No prep work. What is not to like? I should have started this years ago.

We should all do this for each other all the time. Get thirty friends together, and everyone can take one day. On that day, you cook like a madwoman for thirty families. You get totally stressed out, but it's only once a month. Come on; who is with me?

I took a picture of my ass and legs today; it's hard to get a good look otherwise. And they look good. I was told they are Playboy Bunny good. Yes, someone else saw it. It is great to get a nice, sexual comment when you've also got time capsules. It's about time, I say. I will take more naked pictures. I love being naked.

My daughter asked me today if I have ever given a blowjob. She said if she is asked, she is going to tell the guy to get another girl to do it. She is definitely Jewish.

On the way home from Saint Louis, we saw a boy being arrested on the side of the road. Jackson asked me if he was going to jail. I did not know. He asked what jail looked like, if prisoners get a bed, and where they go to the bathroom. I answered, "Well, it's a small room with bars, a small cot, and a toilet where everyone sees you pee and poop." I was figuring he would think, *Oh, I hope I never go to jail so that doesn't happen to me.* Instead, he said, "I never want to be a police officer so I don't have to watch someone pee in the jail cell." That kid just thinks differently. He will either be wildly successful or a member of the prison system (sorry, kid), but I'm banking on wildly successful.

Tomorrow is April Fools' Day. One year when I was young, I called my mom to announce I had gotten engaged . . . to my cousin Paul. Just about gave her two heart attacks for two very different reasons. It's about time I gave her another call. . . .

Did I mention that a few weeks ago, Jackson asked me when St. Patrick's Day was because he wanted to catch a leprechaun? I told him they aren't real, and he accused me of lying. Then I broke it to him that Santa and the tooth fairy aren't real either. He accused me of lying about that too. I was trying to keep him out of therapy for believing in fantasies, but now he'll need it for the trauma of being "lied to" by his mom. Sorry for that, too, kid.

Okay, maybe I get why some people don't like me. I assume it's only some. I have great friends, a fantastic career, and scads of self-confidence. I have cancer, but opportunities abound. Positive learning experiences and becoming positively altered.

But please, people. I'm just trying the best I can. Are you going to begrudge the girl with cancer some positive things in her life? Stop being jealous, and get your own good shit.

22

GIVING UP

I was cutting up my sweatshirts well before Jennifer Beals made it cool in *Flashdance*. Something inside me always needed to come out through my hands, through changing the world in some way. My mother's the same way. She's always painting or putting together these beautiful mosaics.

I used to be a dancer, speaking of *Flashdance*. When we were growing up, my sister was into tennis, but dance was my outlet. I liked the way I could get my body to do these amazing things, and I loved the artistic escape it provided.

There was a show on TV called *Solid Gold*. Kind of a follow-up to *Soul Train*, only they had professional dancers perform choreographed routines to the week's top ten pop songs. I liked the music as much as any kid, but I really watched to see those dancers moving with the music and using their bodies to create something that went beyond what you could hear. You couldn't pull me away from *Solid Gold* for dinner or doing homework or anything. I couldn't imagine anything cooler than to be one of those *Solid Gold* dancers.

Later, the dream became performing on Broadway. My parents

used to take us to the theater and musicals, so I would see these lavish productions with music and sets and all those people running around in this tension between chaos and total, magnificent order. I took lessons and did recitals and the whole thing for several years. I was even in a couple companies and danced professionally. There is still a part of me that wishes I'd stuck it out.

Demi Moore beat me to the pottery wheel. That scene in *Ghost* has become so iconic that my kids know what it is even though they know nothing about the movie or the actors. But I saw it, and it looked damn sexy, and I thought I'd give it a try. So I signed up for a class through Joliet Junior College. It was taught by this woman named Juanda at her little hole-in-the-wall studio.

Let me tell you: I fell in love with throwing clay, but it is *not* as easy as it looks in the movie. You're coordinating your feet and hands and trying to get the right texture and malleability in the clay, and you're actually working against the force of the wheel. It takes more hand and arm strength than I realized it would, and to get good at it requires a lot of practice in centering the clay properly and knowing how to pull and squeeze and apply the right pressure at the right time.

That said, it *is* kinda sexy—except for the first few times, when you're pulling the clay all over the place and making a big mess. Which is also kinda like sex.

I got really into pottery and started making bowls and cups and vases for friends as gifts. I was always the type that, when I'd take the kids to craft fairs and they'd see something they liked, I'd pull them aside and say, "Hey, we can totally make that at home." That thing might have cost $25 or even $100 at the fair, but if I thought we could imitate it, I'd easily spend $500 and hours of trial and error to get there. I would so much rather spend $500 on something I knew took a long time to create than on some print or something that could be mass produced, plus I got to have that time with my kids, making a memory that would *not* require therapy.

There was a point when I guess I burned myself out on pottery. Eventually, everyone you know has several of your pieces and seems less excited when they get another one, and then your own home gets pretty full up of things, and how many decorative cups and plates do you really need? For a while, I took my stuff to arts and craft fairs to sell, but that really messed me up. I had calculated my time to be worth about $450 an hour as a chiropractor, but I couldn't get anywhere near that value for selling pottery, and frankly, it started to piss me off. Eventually, it stopped being fun, and I moved on to other things.

A few years ago, however, I discovered a pottery co-op only twenty minutes from my home and got back into it. My co-op fees get me a key and use of the wheel and kiln. You bring your own glazes and tools. It's never busy when I want to go, which is often around eleven o'clock at night or early on a Sunday, and it became my creative sanctuary. That's the lovely thing about creating: to do it well, you have to give yourself over to it, and then you become so in the moment that you can stop thinking about all the other crap going on in your life and in the world.

When I discovered the cancer, though, I had to reconcile with a hard truth: pottery, as hobbies go, can be pretty unhealthy. The clay is made of silicates, and inhaling free silicates can contribute to emphysema or make you susceptible to tuberculosis. Clay contains kaolin, which can clog your lungs. Depending on where it's harvested, clay can also contain asbestos, which of course contributes to cancer. There are ways of aging and "souring" clay that produces molds that can cause respiratory problems.

The glaze also contains silicates, and for a long time, a lot of them had lead that you might inhale in the studio or ingest if it leaked into food you served in your dish. Even so-called lead-safe glazes are safe only in the sense that, fired right, your finished product won't leak lead into your food; you're still exposed in the studio. The colorants may include arsenic, beryllium, cadmium, hexavalent chromium, nickel, or uranium, which are either known to be or suspected of being carcinogens.

Shoot, even throwing clay can cause carpal tunnel or back problems.

If we want to talk about cancer connect-the-dots, you have to look at my pottery hobby. How many hours did I spend in studios, breathing all that shit into my lungs, absorbing it into my bloodstream, and distributing it all around my body? Not every potter gets cancer. I'd guess most don't.

I did.

Pottery had to go. I have my own wheel that was gifted to me by a man who, as it turned out, would be my daughter's flight instructor years later. Weird, huh? Now it sits idle in the basement. My own little memorial to a lovely hobby. It's sad, of course, to lose something like that. But I had a laser focus on winning over cancer, and if it came down to me or the wheel, I knew what I had to do.

Not long after I gave up pottery, though, I got more into sewing clothes for myself and the kids. Or I would buy nice Louis Vuitton purses and then add my own decorations. I've spent thousands of dollars, I'd bet, on some of that stuff that's now collecting dust somewhere. But they were fun to do and totally worth it.

I have to have an outlet. I think we all do. Life can throw all sorts of crap at us, and we can have the best attitude in the world, but at some point, we have to have a way of working out the stress. It is important to have a way to manage stress: breathing, art, exercise, planting your feet in the earth. Find something. It will change your life.

To some extent, though, you're like a sponge. You can absorb and absorb, but at a certain point, you can't take any more without letting go of something. Your body subconsciously knows when it needs to release something, and if you don't give it a way, then it will take matters into its own hands (so to speak). It might come out as being irritable or getting angry with your family or abusing drugs or alcohol or blowing a bunch of money or doing some other destructive thing. Or you could channel it into something creative.

What makes creativity so wonderful and healing, I think, is that it lets you get yourself out of the way. You're not the dam where all the energy gets knotted up anymore; you're a channel the energy flows through. The world keeps doing things to you; things keep happening to you; and here you get to stop having things done to you and do something to the world. And the thing you're doing is making the world a more wonderful and varied place than it was.

Maybe part of what grabs me about art is that it feels like a safe place to let go of that need for control. Or it transforms my sense of control. Like, I can feel in control of the process, but I know I'm not fully in control of the outcome. The material itself pushes back in terms of what it will allow me to do with it. Part of the fun is trying to get it to do new things. I also give up needing to worry about anything outside of that little moment between me and the clay or fabric.

Pottery, in particular, teaches you to give up control. Other potters had to teach me this. When you put so much time and effort into something, you want it to turn out well of course. But when you're working with glazes, there's only so much you can predict. You pick and mix your colors, and you brush it on in such and such a way to get the effect you want, but once it goes into the kiln, it's all heat and chemistry. What you put in doesn't look like the final product; you never know for sure what you'll pull out.

The hard fact of the matter is that a lot of it will not look good—at least, that was my experience. Potters learn how to take this in stride. They learn to smash things they don't like. Like, literally smash them.

I remember pulling a piece out and saying aloud, "Well, here's another for my basement museum of ugly pottery." Because I had a basement museum of ugly pottery; I never threw anything away.

A woman at the wheel looked confused and said, "Why don't you just smash it?"

I laughed in that friendly way you do when someone makes a joke, but she said, "No, really. Just smash it. You've never done that?"

"No," I said with a little embarrassment. How had I not known about this? "I sometimes give them away as white elephant gifts. . . ."

"We all do it. Why not? You don't have to keep everything you make."

As much as I pride myself on doing my own thing, it had never dawned on me this was an acceptable practice in pottery. I'd felt the disappointment of a piece that had exploded in the kiln or shattered during firing, but smashing a finished piece I didn't like was different. Once this woman said it, though, it was like this strange door opened up in my mind, and I walked right through it. I went home that night, found a spot in my basement, took a hammer, and smashed it through the vase.

Let me tell you: It felt *really* good.

I hit one of the larger pieces again, then another, breaking them into tiny shards. Then I looked around me at all the other ugly vases and cups and ewers and plates and thought, *Oh, wow.*

I grabbed another. *Smash.* Another. *Smash.* It was cathartic, letting go of failed work, of the trials that revealed the errors, of the need to remind myself that I was not good enough. What was this unhealthy attachment to ugly things? Like I needed to be brutally honest with myself or punish myself for the things I did that weren't perfect.

You've got to stop holding on to shit. Toxic shit. Bad art. Bad memories. Bad people. Your disease and brokenness. In a paradoxical way, we hold on to ugly things as an act of denial that they are truly ugly. Keeping them around is a way of insisting that they are salvageable or not as bad as we think. Admitting something is ugly and that you don't need to keep it is shockingly difficult, but it's so amazingly symbolic.

Whether I knew it at the time or not, that lesson helped me with the cancer. I never let the cancer take over my whole sense of self such that I would need to hold on to being "a person with cancer." Instead, it was like my tumors were these ugly bowls I wanted to smash and bury in the yard. Be done with them.

That's something I can be grateful to pottery for. I may have had to give up the clay and the wheel and the glazing and the kiln, but it taught me something that I needed in order to get through one of the toughest chapters in my life.

23

HOW TO MISS A DAY OF WORK

MONDAY, APRIL 28, 2014

How do you miss a day of work? You don't, because you don't miss work. It's that simple.

You may take a day off, but you probably planned it at least a week in advance. You don't get sick and call in, though. It just doesn't happen, and you'll fight anyone who thinks you're lying.

How, then, do you explain last Tuesday? You don't like to admit it, but your time capsules, or the treatment for them rather, are getting to you.

You recall a phenomenon called *lysis*. Chemotherapy kills the cancer cells, often very quickly, and those cells enter your bloodstream faster than your kidneys can process them. There's a buildup of uric acid, potassium, and phosphorus that can cause nausea, fatigue, heart palpitations, even hallucinations. It can also cause horrible pain, which is what hit you. The first time, you were home alone. It was evening. A pain grew in your chest until you couldn't breathe, or at least you felt like you couldn't breathe. It came on quickly, when you were in the kitchen, and it had you bent over the counter, trying not to fall over. You called your oncologist, and he told you if you could talk, you were breathing. He said the tumors were lysing, and there were drugs to help with that, including heavy painkillers. You didn't want to take more drugs, but this was the worst pain you had ever felt.

You didn't let that stop you, though. You kept eating well; you kept working out. You were still Wonder Woman.

And then you did something stupid, and it all caught up to you, and now you know how to miss a day of work.

Start on a Monday. It's been a week since your last vitamin C treatment, so you've made an early appointment for that. Drop off your cold caps in the deep freezer while you're there.

Dr. U. is there, and he asks after you, so go ahead and tell him you are pissed. It will sound strange to both of you because you've never said it before. You always say you're excellent. What's different? You are tired. So tired. You have this intense pain. You don't like it, and you are feeling crabby. Cancer has gotten in your way, and it is unacceptable.

Dr. U. will offer you OxyContin for your pain, but you won't like that idea at all—so many drugs! Walk out of the clinic without the script for it. There is, after all, an opioid crisis. You lecture on it. The numbers and prescriptions are climbing, and it is a major source of unnecessary deaths in this country, especially if you are taking them for musculoskeletal pain. (Yes, here is the commercial break for promoting chiropractic care. I can get you the research. We have a much better solution for your pain.)

Next stop is therapy with Celeste. On the way, speak to Spencer and tell him that you want to discuss goals with her. You often set conscious goals, but you don't always set the minigoals you need to get to the big ones. You don't want this year to pass without reaching your goals. Not this year.

Of course, the session will take an unexpected turn, and yet you'll feel it went exactly how it was supposed to.

Celeste will invite you to acknowledge, affirm, and embrace some truths about yourself, things that you have perhaps known for a long time but not really admitted. So, you start talking, and you come up with quite the list. You say:

- I am very different. I do not like rules made by others. I do not follow rules. I am not interested in breaking the law, but I don't like to follow rules—I need to wander.
- I love my children. I want to find a balance between providing for them and finding my free spirit and answering it. I want to fly.
- I want to travel. I want to meet a million different people and learn from them and share and have them leave as fast as they arrived.
- I want intelligent conversations, and I don't want to argue over minutia.
- I want to continue to learn about my capabilities.
- I feel smothered by my neighborhood and the housewives who drink too much at 10:00 a.m.
- I need a home base but should not spend all my time there.
- I have so much to give professionally. I can be the funny, positive healthcare speaker who inspires many and confuses the rest.
- I am so passionate. I want to give to someone who is capable of receiving as much as he also gives.
- I am so thankful for a few of those people: Spencer, Lori,

Kristin, Laura. They have shined. I am thankful for my staff, who take such good care of me at work. I am thankful my parents and sister are with me.

- I am alive and I am well.
- I am creative and thoughtful, and I have this need to spend more time alone that I am going to follow through on.

Celeste will congratulate you on saying it all out loud. You are truly fantastic!

After your session, it's time to get serious about missing work tomorrow. Celeste is only on the second floor, so walk down the hallway and take the nice marble stairs. Oh, but Spencer is texting you, so text him back. You can see where this is going. You didn't before. Phone, texting, walking, stairs.

Down you go. Almost the whole flight. You shouted as you went down and yelped when you banged your knee, but it's a quiet building and no one sees or hears you fall. So, you sit on the floor at the bottom of the stairs for a few minutes, feeling embarrassed and sorry for yourself and getting scared that you won't be able to stand up on your own.

But eventually you stand and, damn, your right knee hurts like a mother, but you're pretty sure it's not broken. You joke to yourself that you need to make yourself some bubble-wrapping pants and you can avoid this in the future. If you can laugh about it, you'll be okay.

When you get home, the chest pain will set in. But, hey, there's no stopping *you*. You drop by your family friend Dr. Phil to get an

X-ray to make sure you didn't break anything. Dr. Phil is great. You've known him forever. He used to caddie for your father, and though he's a podiatrist, he does everything for your family.

You get the word that there's no break or fracture, then stop home to pick up the kids. You take Reese to her drum lesson and the boys to get their baseball pictures taken, which you always think is the biggest scam. You'll pay $70 for a horrible picture that you could have done better with your phone. Some of the kids have their eyes closed or aren't looking at the camera, the lighting is bad—it's so stupid. Next year, you think, you'll charge each team five bucks, shoot the pictures in your front yard, and give them a disk with a hundred shots on it. Granted, you're a little bitter that the woman who owns the company owes you $1,800 from years ago when she was a patient. You wonder if you have the moxie to tell her you'll deduct the ridiculous cost of her photos from her bill.

When you get home, your pain spikes to a ten out of ten. Between your knee and your chest, you won't be able to sleep. Not a wink. Get out of bed at 4:00 a.m. to pee, and on your way back, take off your shirt because it's soaked from night sweats.

You know you're about to pass out, so you scream for Steve, then fall and hit your head on the closet door as you go unconscious. Reese and Steve come running. You come to quickly and become aware of the fact that you haven't been naked in front of Steve for nearly two years. You really don't care, though, because you're woozy and in pain, and it's not exactly a sexy look to be covered in sweat with your boobs hanging halfway down to the floor.

They get you back to bed, and when you wake up, you're a wreck. You're in so much pain, you can't move to roll over, much less get out of bed. You call your doctor. The nurse, Lindsey, says you need to go to the ER, but you fight her about it. You know that if you went, they would run a million tests and pump you full of meds and hold you for three days. It would cost a small fortune, and you would leave with eight new infections you didn't have when you went in.

You call Mike, your doctor friend, the one who suggested you choose chemo, and he says, "You are going to do something you will never do again." He tells you to take 1,000 mg each of Tylenol and Aleve. That's close to opioid levels. Yeah. But you take them, and you call Spencer, and he takes the call because he knows it must be important if you're calling this early in the morning, and he stays on the line with you for thirty or forty minutes while he can hear the pain in your voice drop from a ten to a four. You're so thankful that he's there when you need him and that he doesn't bullshit you by saying it'll be okay or not to worry.

Now, at last, you realize you can't possibly see patients in the morning. You feel wretched, but part of you resists still, doesn't want to give up or admit defeat. Maybe you can grab three-minute naps between patients. You don't cancel.

Except today you will, and it will be the right choice. It was one of the worst days in a life that has had some legitimate horrible things happen, but now you can't say you have perfect attendance anymore.

24

THE CURIOSITY

Chemo day. Lori picks me up as usual. I haven't seen her in two weeks, and I miss hanging with her. She is a rock star and is loyal, and I can count on her—that is difficult to find. Kristin shows up at the clinic just to hang out, and we meet her friend Tom. Tom wants to bring me plants. I don't know what that is all about, but I tell him he's welcome to bring me all the plants in the world as long as he knows I'll probably kill them.

I also meet Linda and her boyfriend, who are sitting in one of the bays across from me. She tells me today she is Linda, but when she wears a wig, she becomes Lola. Linda has breast cancer. She is an artist, a beautiful woman, and a riot. Drops the f-bomb all the time. Embraces her baldness, eats Lori's quinoa, and sits with us for about an hour. She is from Boston and flies in every two weeks. I like her enough to ask her to come in a day early sometime so we can go hang out in the city. I want to give her big earrings. I think they would look fantastic with her bald head.

Lori and Kristin filmed me changing the cold cap. I narrated it like I was doing a makeup tutorial. Lori says I was funny. Maybe we'll post it on YouTube; if it helps one person, it would be worthwhile. Lori wants to do a documentary. Sure, why not? *Wonder Woman vs. Cancer*!

Four chemos down, eight to go, and I have all my hair. It is curly and gray, but it is mine and I am not going to lose it. Dr. Block came by and took my picture in the cap. It is getting a little weird how fascinated he is with it. Dr. U. told me that Dr. Block tells all his patients about me. I gave him permission to give my number to anyone who wants to ask me about it. Totally worth it. $7,000 hair. *Woo-hoo!*

Today, I decided I am having a party on the last day of chemo. I will invite everyone I love to come celebrate completing the course of treatment. We'll eat nut balls and quinoa, and we will take a big picture and laugh and celebrate whatever anyone feels like celebrating. I think it is a brilliant idea. I love my ideas. I might be the only one, but I don't care.

I am walking through cancer, and it does not define me.

25

MEDICINE SUCKS, AND WE TAKE OUR HANDS FOR GRANTED

Why does medicine suck? Because it is used incorrectly. I am a perfect example of drugs gone bad. (I see that on a T-shirt, Kristin. We always talk about printing weird things on T-shirts but never do it.)

Why do we take our hands for granted? Because we use them for so many things, and when they hurt, you realize how much they do to make your day a little bit easier. So, thank your hands today. (That won't be as good on a T-shirt, Kristin. Or maybe it would. It would certainly get people thinking about what the thankful person was doing with their hands that day.)

The misuse of medicine happened a few times during my treatment. It would have happened more except, being the superhero that I am, I saved the day and said no.

During one of my treatments in the middle of my cycle of chemo, my hands started to swell. A lot of edema, or what I call fat-finger syndrome, which is most obvious when you text with those little letters and there is not a word spelled correctly the first six times you type them.

So we reduced the steroids . . . no improvement.

We reduced them again . . . no improvement.

We eliminated them . . . no improvement.

Next logical step was Lasix. My only experience with this drug was in horse racing. It is commonly used illegally to make a horse lighter. I grew up around the racetrack as my father owned racehorses. Good stories for another day. But my doctor recommended it for me, so I tried one per day . . . no improvement. I tried two. I had become the commercial where you are given all these possibilities for symptoms when taking a drug for other symptoms, which then leads you to taking more drugs for the new symptoms and so on and so on.

I got a great one: urinary incontinence. Woo-hoo! So now my fingers were so fat that when I peed all over myself in public, it took me three times as long to unbutton my pants and wipe myself, allowing even more urine to run down the inside of my leg, making it to my calf and if I was really lucky, into my shoe, which, if they were cowboy boots, was a blessing because they collected the urine, whereas flip-flops just became slippery, and then not only did I piss myself, but I had to have someone help me up after I slipped into a puddle of my own urine while they exclaimed, "Hey, can anyone else smell pee?"

If anyone reading this works for an ad agency that does drug commercials, can you let me know if there is a market for this story? I would love to star in a commercial about drugs gone bad. "I'm Cindy. Have you ever slipped in a puddle of your own pee? Then you know it's no fun." And so on.

As if you had to ask, I stopped taking the drug. A week later, I stopped peeing all over myself. What do you know? Thankfully, that side effect is reversible.

Urine is a funny thing. We all produce it, and we're happy to release it into pools and the ocean, but otherwise we don't want to walk around in it.

I couldn't open a water bottle by myself on some days. I dropped things all the time. I had my ten-year-old son shift my gears in the car when it was below 60° outside. My fingers turned white and felt like they were frostbitten. My livelihood was affected, as I had trouble performing chiropractic manipulation first thing in the morning. I had trouble getting my rings on and off. A manicure didn't always feel good anymore. I texted weird, obscene, and nonsensical things because after typing the same word wrong six times, I got frustrated, no longer cared, and sent the message anyway. The drug companies need to read my book and create a new drug to help with this new condition called fat-finger syndrome. Maybe with the new one, I would poop in my pants instead.

"Hi, I'm Cindy, and I suffer from fat-finger syndrome. Blah-dee-blah-dee-blah reduced the swelling so I wasn't texting inappropriate words to my ex-husband. Blah-dee-blah-dee-blah may cause pooping in your pants, but take it from me; that's easier to manage than peeing yourself." Big smile!

> *I am healthy, but my hands hurt. I believe it is a*
> *side effect of the chemo gone bad in my body, as I*
> *have never had it before. Hypoxia, vasospasm,*
> *Raynaud's—all rare side effects of chemo. So, I start-*
> *ed a protocol. Natural supplementation, of course.*
> *Only on it for a few days, so I will let you know*
> *how it works. My oncologist read an article that a*

calcium channel blocker is the drug of choice. Will it
make me pee down my leg? Then I am not taking it.
I will wear gloves and use hand warmers and stay
off gluten and take supplements and eat well and
exercise and yell and scream when they hurt, but I
will fix this. I don't hope it will go away; I will make
it go away.

Cancer taught me a ton of things: One, I didn't make changes in my life because I experienced cancer. I made changes in my life because it was time. I was coasting, and even with coasting, you eventually run out of gas. It just occurs more slowly. What I found was that I was bored, bitter, and unhappy. What I then found was that I love traveling and meeting new people and life in general. There is so much to explore.

What I also learned is to live in the moment. So many of us don't know how to do this. We worry about later and next year or how we will get through tomorrow. While tomorrow is bound to happen for most of us, what creates happiness for me is to stop and look around exactly where I am and find happiness in the moment. Right now, happiness comes from looking at the Atlantic Ocean. Earlier today, it came from feeling the sun on my untanned body. This morning, it was, well, that's my own private moment.

The point is that we can miss the many things there are to appreciate and notice if we aren't focused on the present. How does that meal taste? Is there a flower or a seashell you would have just walked by? Our surroundings are so beautiful; stop and notice. Every night that I can look at the sunset, the colors, the clouds, the texture, the distance between us and the sun is a night I wasn't guaranteed a year ago. It is amazing. And for those few moments, nothing else exists—no work, no stress, no illness. Try it.

Earlier I asked you to stop what you were doing and dance. I know most of you didn't do that, so here is your second chance. Check out the sunset tonight. No one looks at you funny if you do.

I also learned that I shouldn't wait to do anything. Now is the best and only time because I don't actually know what tomorrow will bring or what I will be in the mood for or if the world is coming to an end as some people believe may happen on any given day. There is always more money; there is not always more time. Love, laugh, be silly, and be nice to someone. It is amazing how you are rewarded when you pay someone else a compliment or just pay for their coffee. Look at Facebook: when someone ahead of you at Starbucks picks up the tab, then you beam about it all day.

I have a fabulous life. My mom is terminal, the dog died, I left my husband, and I am experiencing Hodgkin's lymphoma (I'll have to have screenings the rest of my life). I have the sob story, and I have already told you this. Nonetheless, my life is fantastic. I have the most amazing man in my life. Get one of those, or a woman or a child or a robot. Find someone who complements you and challenges you to grow. I enjoy every day. I laugh at least once a day, especially at myself, and usually more. I look at what's around me, and I can't wait to see what is next.

26

CONVERSATIONS WITH DR. BLOCK

The day I completed my sixth chemo treatment—the last of the third cycle and halfway through the program—Dr. Block came by to talk. I guess he likes getting into fights about treatment with me.

He still likes to take pictures of me in my cold cap. I don't know if he's planning to encourage other patients to try them or if he just has a weird thing for women with ugly blue wraps on their heads freezing their follicles. He told me he needs to bring his checkbook so he can pay me for using my picture. That sounds right to me.

He asked about my symptoms, and I said, "They're pissing me off."

"Is that right?" he asked, though he knew by now what I would say.

"I still have a lot of pain in my chest and neck, and it's really getting in the way."

"Well, cancer will do that. Your numbers look great, though. The Neulasta is working."

Hahahaha! I'm not taking the Neulasta! I debated whether I should tell him, then decided to give him my truth.

"No, it's not; I'm not taking the Neulasta. Once was enough with that stuff. No, thank you. Never again." I had debilitating back pain for three days after the first dose.

He sighed, but I could tell from his smirk that he wasn't surprised.

"I know you had some side effects," he said. "We can manage that. But we have to protect you from infections."

"That's all right," I told him. "I'm managing that my own way."

"You know," he said, "if it was a member of my family going through chemo, I would hold them down in the chair to get their shot."

"Good thing we aren't related," I said. Anyway, Lori and I could take him between us. Come at me, Dr. Block! I dare you.

"Well, your numbers are good," he said. "I take some credit for that. We're doing all the right things."

"Hey, I take all the credit," I shot back. Aren't I a fun patient to have? "I came in here working out, eating perfectly, and knowing what supplements I needed and what IV nutrients I wanted. You're the facilitator, sure, but I want the credit!"

I'm glad he likes me because I can say this kind of crap to him and he laughs instead of getting mad. Anyway, I'm right. We physicians facilitate and educate, but the patient should have the final say about her body and her health.

I found out they have IV curcumin, a therapy using a compound found in turmeric that can treat inflammation. I asked Dr. Block for some to help with the pain from the tumor lysis.

He told me, "You're not paying attention! You have a curable cancer, and we're making good progress. I don't want to change the protocol at this stage."

"How about we compromise. I'll have it as soon as I am done to clear out the effects of the chemo and then after each PET scan to help decrease inflammation."

"That works for me," he said. "You're a smart one."

"I know!"

And I want to use what I know and what makes sense to help me heal.

May 28, 2014

Fighting with Dr. Block aside, today was a tougher day than most. I am sick of treatment being in my way. That is just a mindset, because everything can get in the way if you let it. It is all about choice. The choice to do something. The choice to view every activity as one that can be an obstacle or a benefit or just an activity that is a means to accomplish something else.

27

EXCUSES

MAY 31, 2014

I got a kick in the butt today that I didn't even know I needed. I was on the phone with Spencer, explaining all the reasons I haven't been training the same as before my diagnosis and why I can justify a little bit of ginger ale to help with nausea because I won't take any more meds.

Spencer told me to stop with the bullshit—yes, he said *bullshit*. Normally, he says vulgarity is the crutch of the verbally weak, so I knew he was being serious. Anyway, I know plenty of big words; does that make me a vulgar intellectual? He told me to do what I do, which is what no one else does because I am me and I am capable. It is just a matter of making the decision to do it and to stop finding reasons not to.

Here is what is fascinating for me: I know I am doing better than most people going through cancer treatment. I know my attitude is good. I know that I still sometimes fall into the realm of "Well, I can't do everything because I am affected by treatment."

Here is what I also know. That is bullshit. I have chosen not to do some of those things. It is always about choice. I chose not to work out and train like I used to because I rationalized that I can get my muscles back but not my life.

I am not dying, but I am also not living up to my potential. Tomorrow I will get up at 4:00 a.m., and I will go to the gym. I emailed Bob for some of the HIIT workouts I was doing so that I can start them in the gym. I texted to set up private training to learn new things. And tomorrow I will text Spencer to tell him I am in the gym doing legs. It's exciting, and all it took was a good kick in the butt from a dear man who sees through my bullshit even when I don't. If you don't have a friend like that, become one so that someone returns the favor. The best friends in the world will call you out and challenge you so that you don't get lost in excuses and you can rise above all the excuses to succeed.

I am not cancer. It does not define me. It is not me. I am Cindy, a brave, strong, intelligent, funny, silly, healthy, strong, sexy, motivated woman!

28

MAYBE CANCER WILL HELP

My friend's son has survived brain cancer. He is now fourteen. In his short life, he has been through more struggles than most will go through in a lifetime. He is five foot one, and his doctors say he might grow another inch, but that is it. He is not bitter; in fact, he's a great kid. I say he is five foot one of fabulous.

We constantly strive for outside validation. Why did we become a people who measure our self-worth based on our home, our job, our toys, our vacations, and most importantly, what other people think? Why is it so hard to find internal validation? Get cancer; maybe that will help. It helped me. I am beautiful, and yet I am the oldest I have ever been. I am starting to get crow's-feet when I squint, and the C-section scar makes my stomach look like a second ass. I have fewer friends than I have ever had. I am not worth millions (but I will be). I got rid of the boat. The coolest toy I have is a two-inch tractor that I soldered myself this year in a welding class. I don't receive daily compliments. I don't hear from G-d, and no one takes care of me. So how is it possible that I feel great and that I truly mean I am fantastic when you ask me how I am?

I honor the little things. What is important doesn't have to be grandiose—you just need to give the little joys the attention that they deserve. I love the feel of grass under my feet and water rushing around my ankles on the beach. I love when my dad now tells me he is proud of me and I did a good job raising my kids. I love getting a random text from my daughter that says she misses me. I love when my sons lose a wrestling match only because I know they are getting stronger internally and it is making them better men; I really love it more when they win. I love that dairy-free ice cream now comes in yummy flavors. I love thong underwear; I spent too many years picking a pair of undies out of my butt—now it just stays there. I love fresh flowers in my bedroom because they make me feel special. Well, they can't make me feel anything, but I am special enough to buy them for myself. I love a warm cup of tea in front of a fireplace when it is frigid outside.

I have turned to quiet, patience, joy, and forgiveness. I forgive myself for not getting through my to-do list that now has its own to-do list. More importantly, I forgive myself for not being perfect. Instead, I have chosen to strive for excellence. It is a lifelong journey, and that is so exciting because my growth never ends and I can always improve. How cool is that? Someone told me once that if it's not okay, then it isn't the end. How profound those words have been for me. Life does not end with a perceived bad event. It provides an opportunity to see how you choose to approach it and conquer it. I read something the other day—I can't remember where; I still have a little chemo brain left—and it asked me for my favorite word. After mulling it over for a few days, I realized what it is: *choice*. As in, we always have a choice in everything. I have chosen wisely this last year.

What would it look like if we chose to be resilient in every aspect of our lives?

Stop reading for a moment, put this down, and ask yourself this question out loud. What would it look like if I was resilient in every aspect of my life?

I'm fascinated by studies where athletes who visualized themselves in a contest outperformed those who practiced for the contest. Why? Because when the athletes visualized the contest, they always won; they saw victory; their brains didn't visualize failure. And the neuroplasticity of the brain holds on to this information and uses it successfully when competing. What would it look like if we visualized everything we wanted in life? Would we win that contest? I believe we would.

Spencer and I had a conversation about him becoming an expert in concussion for our profession. He kept telling me it was what he wanted. I told him he already was an expert, and that instead of saying, "I want," he should say, "I am." A few weeks later, he got a call from our national organization's executive vice president asking him if he could testify in Ohio as an expert in concussion. I loved saying I told you so. It's childish, but it proves my point. We are what we say we are.

We believe ourselves, so speak kindly and with excellence. Write down what you are (in most cases what you want to be), and become it. Read it out loud. Write it with lipstick on your mirror in your bathroom. Shout it out your window and scare the neighbors. Even if you're wearing a cold cap (especially if you're wearing a cold cap). It will become contagious. Hang out with the five people you most want to be like. If you are the smartest person in the room, get out and find another room so you can learn something. Never finish a day without experiencing something fun. Laugh, cry, acknowledge, live, and be resilient and excellent.

29

LAST DAY OF TREATMENT

My last day of treatment was August 27, 2014, one week later than planned because I took Ari to Hollywood (the Florida one, again) for his birthday, which I will always cherish and be grateful that I could do.

At the Block Center, we celebrated. Balloons, flowers, and the Benadryl dance. It's a whole thing. An allergic reaction to the Emend and huge hugs for Dr. U. and for Lori and for my nurse and for me.

It was actually pretty anticlimactic.

30

THE CANCER DIDN'T KILL ME, BUT THE AIR MIGHT

SEPTEMBER 2, 2014

It is hard to kill the people in my family. We have close calls and narrow escapes, but we survive and go on and live until we are one hundred years old.

I've had several brushes with death myself. One, of course, was during Reese's birth, when I almost bled out in the delivery room. No need to relive that trauma again.

The others are less gory but have their drama. The two that really stick out happened in my car. I drive fast. Like, recklessly fast. I have things to do and places to be; I hate being in the car where I can't really do anything but sit. On one occasion, we were driving to Minneapolis. It was Steve, myself, and our first dog, Boomer, who was in the back of the SUV. The roads were horrible because it was snowing heavily and ice was forming. I was in the far-left lane of the highway when I hit a patch of ice. It sent us sliding right all the way across the highway until we hit a pole or something, which bounced us left all the way back—right in front of a semitruck. We were spinning, and the truck was coming right at us, trying to brake, and I could see that big grill bearing down on us. We missed it by what felt like inches and wound up in the center median, breathless and pretty sure someone had to be watching out for us.

Another time, I was also heading north, this time to meet Frank, my friend and mentor, for a day of salmon fishing. It was early, around 4:30 a.m., and I was on I-294, driving fast in the left lane, as usual, and enjoying the fact that there was no traffic, which is a rare occurrence at any time. So, there are almost no cars, and I'm flying on my way to have a nice day, and something compels me to suddenly slow down and switch lanes to get right behind another car. This is something I would never do under normal circumstances, but for some reason that morning it felt like the thing to do. Maybe part of my unconscious brain noticed something my conscious brain did not, because within seconds, a car came barreling down that lane in the wrong direction, right where I had just been.

It's moments like that that make me say I should be dead. Only, if I should be dead, I would be dead, but I'm not, so I *shouldn't* be dead, and it's a stupid thing to say.

But I should be dead. In fact, I almost killed myself six nights ago. I mean, I really almost killed myself. To be very clear, I wasn't suicidal. It was the evening before my last treatment for the Hodgkin's lymphoma that I no longer have. I had been running IV vitamin C for six months at home, and that night should have been no different. However, it was.

Have you ever had the feeling that you needed to immediately tell three little people that you love and adore them and you are sorry you are leaving them motherless and you hope your friend Kristin will marry their dad and take care of them knowing that you really don't want her to marry their dad and not because you are jealous but because there is no way you want her to take care of him like you have for seventeen years?

No? Just me?

I talked to Kristin the other day, and she promised me she would take care of my kids without marrying my ex. *Phew!*

Almost killing myself led to a very late night, a great pajama party and sleepover in my bedroom, and a week's worth of tripping over pillows and blankets, because now that I am alive, there is no reason they should clean up the sleepover mess. I have a renewed purpose, and part of that involves the continuous cleanup after my kids, I guess.

I wonder if when I'm dead, I will be able to scream at the top of my lungs from the fiery hell where I am partying with my best friends loud enough for the kids to hear me. Bummer, guess I'm not finding out this week. The kids still have a mom. I still have a soon-to-be ex-husband, and I have my life. What is most important is I have happiness; I have a purpose; I have a reason to live; and I am pretty confident that I will never kill anyone else in the way I almost killed myself.

So, how did I almost do it? No overdose, no great story, no car accident—nothing glamorous could take my life. Nope, this is a story about an IV vitamin C drip, the very drip that has helped keep me healthy through the course of my treatment. Wouldn't it be ironic if I died the night before my last chemo treatment—*after* I beat cancer? How would that eulogy go? "She was so brave, so strong, and had the most amazing attitude, but dang, an air bubble killed her. Tough luck, kiddo. But look at her hair. Isn't it fabulous? If you like the curtains, you should see the floor. It's been newly waxed." (People don't usually ask me to write eulogies.)

I sat down and got my IV bag ready, but this time it was different. The bag holds 500 ml of sterile water. I usually use 250 ml, but instead of doubling my dosage, I got rid of half the fluid, first by running it through the line and then just squeezing it out of the bag. When I hooked the line back up, however, I did not run the fluid through it or bleed the line. As a result, there was air in the line, and I did not notice it.

Do you know what happens when an air bubble gets into your vein? No, it doesn't help you choke a vampire. It's called a *venous air embolism*, but it might as well be called a venomous embolism. That harmless-looking bubble can travel to your brain and cause a stroke, or to your heart and cause a heart attack, or to your lungs and cause lung failure. In other words, you can die. You can die quickly. A little air bubble like that can literally kill you.

I have joked with people about chemo brain throughout this whole process, but now it had become potentially life-threatening, and that just wasn't funny. Steve was there, and he actually was the one who stuck the needle into my arm. Then he rolled the stop back on the line, and the nutrients began to flow. But then I noticed something: It was like something rushing into me, and the noise scared me. A giant *whoosh. OMG. I didn't bleed the line,* I thought to myself as I started shaking with the worst fear I have ever had and a shortness of breath that might have been real because I was dying or because I was hyperventilating or because my kids would see me die when I'd promised I would be fine after cancer (which, by the way, was a dumb thing to promise because it might not have happened. Add it to my list of shouldn't haves). My heart rate was about 200 bpm. Anything over 85 is a concern.

"Steve, call Mike Taylor," I yelled, referring to the same physician friend who talked me into chemo all those months ago. "There's air in the line!"

He grabbed his phone, and it was like he couldn't dial fast enough because I might die while he needed to remember each number one by one, and he said, "I think you will be all right." Which was not the right thing to say. The idea that I would be okay was no less obvious than if a psycho cut off your legs with a butcher knife and someone said, "Oh, that's okay; you can grow two new ones."

Luckily, thankfully, Mike answered. *It is not my turn to die*, I thought. You can't kill my family. There have been multiple attempts on three of the four of us, but it's just not in our cards yet. Still, Mike confirmed that I was in trouble, and it's scary when the person you're entrusting with your life is also scared.

"Lie down on your left side, head down, and elevate your butt six inches above your head, and just stay like that for the next six hours," he instructed us. We needed to make sure the air traveled to my butt and not my head or . . . I could die.

Do you have any idea how uncomfortable it is to lie on your left side with your butt six inches higher than your head? Give it a try for just five minutes and report back to me. It is horrible. Everyone stayed in the room with me—Steve and the kids, that is. I suppose they either wanted to make sure I didn't roll over and die, or they hoped to be the first to go through my jewelry so they could sell it for cash after I was gone. I wouldn't put it past Steve to have thought something like that. Maybe Ari, too; he's practical that way. At some point, I called Kristin so I could hear another trusted adult voice. Kristin wouldn't rush for my jewelry at least.

It was a long evening of just lying there, waiting. What we were waiting for was not some specific event. Rather, we were waiting in hopes that nothing would happen. As time dragged on and nothing happened, the kids started to feel more confident that things would be okay, and they were in and out of the room. Me? I wasn't going to move until the clock hit that six-hour mark. Maybe not for a little while after that.

Mike said if you get air in one-third of the line, you are in trouble. The next day, he told me that less than that could have done it. I don't care if it was a centimeter of air; I didn't want to go out that way, not after all that trouble over the cancer.

But I am alive, and I get to keep my jewelry.

31

TOP-TEN LISTS

Ten most memorable events, people things, events in my whole life:

1. Birth of Reese
2. Birth of Ari
3. Birth of Jackson
4. My grandma Ruth
5. Being with my great-grandma when she passed away at 103
6. Dancing professionally onstage
7. Graduating from U of Wisconsin
8. My very first chiropractic patient
9. The true friendship of a few people in the past year
10. The Rick Springfield concert
11. My very first love (That's eleven. Sue me.)

Ten most life-changing events:

1. Birth of my first child
2. Marriage
3. The suicide attempt of my fiancé
4. The first time I had sex
5. My mother's diagnosis of multiple myeloma
6. My diagnosis of Hodgkin's lymphoma
7. One morning in Florida (the air-conditioning guy, the fishermen, and the lady with purple hair—a story for another time)
8. The day I decided to leave my husband
9. Realizing I don't fit in and that I am extremely unique and accepting that

(One short of ten, but it balances out the extra one from the previous list.)

32

BARBADOS

(IT DOESN'T MATTER WHAT DAY IT IS; I'M ON A BEACH)

Everyone should have a Barbados. This is my first time here, and it is just beautiful. I have never had a Barbados. Two weeks before, a friend invited me to vacation with her. It was a bit last minute, and at first, I kept trying to make excuses for why I shouldn't go. That's actually a big step from what I used to do, which was try to talk myself into going. Years ago—heck, even months ago—I would not have cleared my schedule to say yes as I would have felt irresponsible. Now, I think it's irresponsible not to say yes. I have a wandering spirit, and I need to nurture it.

People like to fantasize about picking up and going to the airport and hopping on the next plane going out and just leaving everything behind for a bit. That's Barbados. The world will not come to an end if you say yes or just go, and if it does, well then, this is the place to be when it ends. Bury me in the ocean off the most beautiful place, Crane Beach. I am good with that.

This now makes me rethink rules and why I have always defied them or at least wanted to on a very deep level. I am not sure who makes them up and what qualifies them in their own mind to do so. I do agree with the "thou shall not kill" one, but other than that, I am pretty open.

33

HAPPY CHINESE TAKEOUT DAY

DECEMBER 25, 2014

Happy Chinese Takeout Day! That's the Jewish version of "Merry Christmas." When I was a child, we were either in the car arriving in Florida or on a plane riding the clouds to Florida or already in Florida and wondering why the only open restaurants were Chinese. Let me rephrase that: pseudo-Chinese, as they served American Chinese cuisine.

I do think I recall Little Caesars Pizza being open one year. It was such a great deal for Jews. You got two square pizzas for the price of one. We love a bargain—we would pay a million bucks for a thing if it had been marked down from two million bucks—and there is nothing cooler in the pizza world than two square pizzas. I think a triangular pizza would be cool. Or a pizza place in which any shape is obtainable and really talented cheese-eating, sausage-shaping, pepperoni-flinging enthusiasts can create their own shape for the additional charge of $9.99.

It's Christmas Day in 2014, and I am staying at Butch and

Susan's house in the Gold Coast neighborhood of Chicago. I've known this couple for most of my life; they were great friends of my parents, and I treasure them. It is a beautiful 46°F, which some may classify as a heat wave for this time of year. I decided to go for a walk and do some people-watching after spending hours writing a presentation called "Small Intestinal Bacterial Overgrowth." By now you know anything that can lead to a conversation about poop is a subject worth mentioning at even the most elegant events.

I walk east, not even a block, to Michigan Avenue, home of Montblanc and Tiffany & Co, and I immediately pass an older gentleman who wishes me a Merry Christmas. I kindly say thank you and reciprocate. Now, here is the ridiculous thought that traversed my brain. Did he wish me a Merry Christmas because he celebrates Christmas and assumed I did too? Or was he Jewish and assumed I was not and was just being polite? Did we just have two Jews wishing one another a Merry Christmas? This makes me think further because I cannot just let one thought in and not have it morph into something greater. Why do we say typical things that we expect people will want to hear?

A friend told me today that I was liked, I was loved, and I was not able to be withstood. If that wasn't pure raw honesty, I don't know what is. Why are we so incapable of sharing the raw pure thoughts that we truly have with those we like, love, and can't stand?

The ability to communicate and speak openly and honestly is lost in most cases. Turn to whoever is near you and tell them exactly how you feel about them right now. It's a little scary, but it is so empowering and rewarding, and what will happen is you will find yourself surrounded with those people who will challenge you and embrace you out of love and passion for making you a better version of your already fabulous self. I am in this fantastic place—one of confidence, security, self-love, joy, and brilliance because of this. I am every day a better version of me, which beats being a better version of anyone else. Ask yourself: *Who do I want to be?* And if you say Gandhi or Madonna or Ricky Martin, you are missing the point. You should say, "I am me, and I am fabulous!"

We were in Florida only a few days ago. I took my three kids and three friends on a thrill ride in a powerboat in Miami. We passed Ricky Martin's house and Shaq's and Gloria Estefan's and . . . who gives a crap? Really, do people get impressed by this? They are structures that someone paid for, poops in, and probably has at least ten pairs of shoes in the closet. Does that make it impressive? I have always said that I am impressed because you are impressive and not because you tell me how impressive you are. Please don't tell me about the ball on top of Ricky Martin's home. It looks ridiculous; it doesn't mean anything with any substance; and really, does anyone care? And if they do, please make sure they do not enter my circle of friends as I have no time for silly minutia such as that.

It's okay if you like me but can't stand me. I get it.

34

PREMIER PASSENGER

I am now a premier something-something member on Southwest Airlines. Big deal. What that means is I fly too much, and they rewarded me with the ability to board in the first group regardless of the boarding number I draw. I also get to go into a different line to check in, but I still get to look ridiculous when my suitcase weighs fifty-four pounds (oh, and that is when I am only traveling for three days), so I throw my thongs around, trying to take out four pounds of straight irons, bras, and cowboy boots to put into a separate bag so I don't have to pay extra money because my bag is four pounds too heavy.

Here's a warped thought (yes, I know most of my thoughts are warped): everything is about weight with an airplane. With so much fuel, we can take so much weight such and such a distance. Whether I bring one bag or two, I still bring the same poundage, so that shouldn't matter. What if when we bought tickets, we registered our current weights, and if I am flying with a bunch of skinny people, they send me an email the day before and say, "Congrats! You can bring your dumbbells in your suitcase this trip because no one on your flight drinks Frappuccino something-somethings from Starbucks or knows what a cookie is."

If it is a bunch of heavy people, the email would look something like, "Ooh, so sorry. Your flight is so heavy, no one can bring a bag at all, so wear two thongs tomorrow under your favorite pair of jeans when you travel and be prepared to wear them inside-out on the way back."

Better yet, charge me ten more bucks; hire people who can lift one hundred pounds so we don't kill trees printing tags that say, "Careful; this bag is too fricking heavy," and let me bring the seventeen pairs of shoes on my three-day trip so I can change five times a day and still have two extra pairs just in case.

Actually, I wonder if just leaving my vibrator at home would have kept my bag under fifty pounds. No, that thing can't weigh that much.

While writing the final draft of this book, I came across an email from the MD Anderson Cancer Center. On the banner across the top, the word *cancer* in their logo had a red strike through it, and the newsletter was called *Cancerwise*. Finally, someone else gets it about the naming conventions. I will send them a copy of this book.

Enough time has passed that some of those places that played such an important role in my walk through cancer feel like other worlds I once visited on a really crummy adventure. The Block Center. That majestic U of C hospital. The bland pre-op room where I told Lori about the letter I had written to my kids. I wonder what happened to that letter?

A study revealed that the kind of face a woman finds attractive on a man can differ depending on where she is in her menstrual cycle. For example, if she is ovulating, she is attracted to men with rugged and masculine features. However, if she is menstruating or menopausal, she tends to be more attracted to a man with duct tape over his mouth and a spear lodged in his chest while he is on fire. No further studies are expected on this subject, though I do wonder if I could tolerate a penis if it was covered in duct tape.

Oh, and I've taken up photography! You know, no chemicals. The details like ISO and shutter speed confuse me, though, so sometimes my pictures rock and sometimes they flat out suck. I bought the camera to give me something to do at my boys' wrestling matches other than jumping up and down and screaming. I figured I couldn't focus on taking a great picture and act like a madwoman at the same time. That much is true. Instead, I jump and scream like a madwoman while taking crappy pictures.

This is Cindy.

Cindy goes to a concert or a wrestling tournament or Barbados and enjoys every moment of the show instead of taking thousands of pictures with the dumb phone. Cindy goes to Barbados because she saw an Instagram post that said, "Seize the moment!" or something cliché like that, and she has a great time in Barbados and drinks too much rum out of a coconut she bought from a tamale vendor on the street.

Cindy is smart. Cindy is brave and funny and amazing—Wonder

Woman. Cindy is walking through cancer, but she feels great. There were times she did not feel great at all, but she refused to give up and refused to let cancer tell her how to feel, and she made it to the other side of treatment and is taking care of herself so she can live to 112.

Be like Cindy. Actually, be you.

Or be whoever you want to be. My journey through cancer and through life will never be duplicated. Hopefully some of it resonated with you or made you laugh; maybe some of it was hard to swallow, for good or ill. If it got a response at all, that's fantastic. The only way you could make me sad is if you didn't read past the first page and learn anything more about my story.

I love that we all have a journey. I have loved mine. I would do it all over again. Honestly, I would. I might change a couple things. Like, I would copyright the name Karen or take more photos of my hair. I would have loved a bit harder, breathed a bit deeper, and bought more flowers. (I do love flowers.) I . . .

Okay, I'm back. I literally had to stop and breathe and admire the flowering trees outside my window. I was saying, it can still be challenging to live in the moment, but I'm better at it now than I've ever been.

My new favorite day of the year is today. Every today is my new favorite. It could be yours too.

POSTSCRIPT

VALENTINE'S DAY

FEBRUARY 14, 2021

One of the ladies in my book club told us her husband has been diagnosed with lung cancer. I know him as a Facebook friend more than anything. He shared his diagnosis there and said he was going to fight and asked that if anyone saw him, to say, "You got this." Then he declared his spirit warrior was Iron Man.

Last I checked, there were over five hundred comments on the post, all supporting and encouraging him. Usually, I respond to those things, but this time I didn't. Instead, I contacted him on Messenger. I wrote:

> Hi, Kevin. I just read your post. My spirit warrior was Wonder Woman when I walked through Hodgkin's lymphoma six and a half years ago. Just as a body sometimes gives in, the body is also an amazingly strong tool. It can overpower anything. I wanted to pass along a thought. I was challenged

by a close friend when I diagnosed myself to never say the words, "I am sick." She challenged me to say, "I am walking through it" or "experiencing it," and that is exactly what I did. I walked through and experienced Hodgkin's lymphoma, with all its struggles and all its beauty. I welcomed it into my life so I could get to the other side of a fantastic journey. What is truly amazing is there are some really unique gifts that you are going to now experience. Welcome those, too; they really are unbelievable. On your journey, if there's anything I can do to support you nutritionally or if you want to run questions by me from a medical standpoint, I would be happy to give you my two cents from a more holistic approach. Please feel free to reach out as that definitely helped me get through my experience.

He replied with such gratitude, and I wanted to hear from him. It felt good to touch even one person before this book was in its final stages. My work is complete.

Update: Kevin passed away, ultimately, not long after his diagnosis. We all feel that he left a great legacy, a shorter journey than mine, I thought. Though his cancer journey was shorter than mine, I thought he was even more positive than I had been. It was inspiring and beautiful. Cancer can be conquered, but not all the time. Kevin didn't let it define him, didn't let it become the whole or only story.

POST-POSTSCRIPT

SIX YEARS LATER

MARCH 8, 2021

It is the evening before my fifty-second birthday, and I am feeling low. I act like I like birthdays, but the truth is, most of them have been a disappointment. Sometimes people or events let me down, but sometimes I expect too much from the day, give it too much importance. That's weird for me, right? The woman who questions every other weird social convention just buys right into the "birthdays are special days for me" thing. It's really just another day, a day that comes after the day before and before the day that comes after.

I'm sitting here in my room, in my chair, on the cowskin rug, thinking about my birthday and finishing this book. On the table next to me is a photo of my three kids, and on the wall near that is a painting of the ocean Reese made. Past that, my lazy dog, Walter, snores on my bed, and out the window over the bed, I can see a magnificent sunset. The faces of my kids, the texture of the paint, the peacefulness of my dog, the layers of color in the sky . . . it's all so beautiful. I still remember to find beauty every day, even when I'm feeling low. If there's a depth from which beauty can't provide some relief, I haven't found it, and I hope I never do.

The other day, my friend Jay asked his HealthTech Tribe Facebook group, "What's the *one* most important thing you are going to accomplish next week?" Seeing all the great answers really pumped me up, and I had a to-do list for my to-do list with items that would have made great answers too. What I wrote, however, was, "I am going to celebrate my fifty-second birthday with gratitude for my health, my friends, and my family." That's most appropriate to me, more so than starting a new corporation or launching a new project or whatever. All good things, and things I might do, but I want to always work on the small, the simple, like the beauty, the love, of seeing those colors out my window that will never appear in quite the same way again. Like the helicopter ride in Sedona. It's funny; I just talked to Christina, my helicopter-ride buddy, today. Life keeps circling back around like that.

Can you believe it's been six and a half years since my last treatment? Well, believe it. I told you I was going to get through it, and I did. Five years is the big anniversary people talk about. That's what the cancer survival curves always look at. If you can make it five years, you have a much higher chance of making it longer. For Hodgkin's, five years on this side of the soil is considered "cured." August 27, 2019, was my five-year anniversary of my last day of treatment. My boyfriend, Keith, my kids, and I made plans to meet for dinner at Francesca's, the restaurant that knows my name. I wanted to mark it in some way, and I thought having the most important people in my life there, even for a small dinner, would be enough.

When I arrived at Francesca's, they said my party was already there and led me back toward the curtain that separated the private dining room from the main hall. When they pulled the curtain back, I saw a long table of family and friends who had come out to celebrate me. I was stunned. Speechless, which is saying a lot for me. It turned out I had more feelings than I had realized, gratitude and happiness and love that opened up because I was surrounded by it. If my life were a movie, it would have been the most cliché moment, but as the woman who lived it, I can tell you it was deeply meaningful.

My mom is still with us too. When I ask her how she's doing, she says, "I am cured!" I get my strength and my attitude from my mom. Sarcasm and PMA ("positive mental attitude"), that's my mom. A few months ago, I was on a podcast and was asked who my hero was. I could have said any number of famous or professional people, but I blurted out, "My mom!" My cancer journey had a good prognosis; what she has . . . there's not much light at the end of her tunnel. Yet she is determined to see her grandkids grow up, and she makes the most of every day. We've decided that when she passes, she'll come back as a pink flamingo, so keep an eye out. If you see a pink, long-legged bird strolling down Lake Shore Drive in the middle of a Chicago winter, then we can know for sure we come back around again to visit our loved ones. If you don't see any flamingos on Lake Shore Drive, do not worry; my mom will also be making an appearance in my upcoming book, which is already in the works.

Every year, I have a greater appreciation of my parents. That's how it's supposed to go, right? In retrospect, I can see that they did everything they could, in the moment, to be amazing parents—just like I do. And just like me, they didn't have a manual. Sure, we can all see how we could have done things differently, but we can't beat ourselves up over that. My sister and I laugh about so much of it now, though my parents claim they don't remember things the way we do. "Your Honor, we have no recollection of events as the witness reports them, so they must not have happened that way." Sure, Mom. I'm lucky to have my parents, and I'm lucky to have a little sister who puts up with my sarcasm, my stubbornness, my attitude, all of it. I love you, Lisa, and I love that you're the best tante to my kids!

When I look at my kids, I think about how much bigger they are than when this all started. I'm now third in line in terms of height. Ari is seventeen years old and five foot eleven—"big and juicy," as he puts it. Somehow, I don't think he'll like me putting it that way, though. He spends two to three hours a day in our basement gym, and he's already beat my personal records for deadlift (315 pounds), squats (315 pounds), and bench press (165 pounds). That means I have a new goal in life: to out-lift him. My car sits in the driveway because he's building skateboard ramps in the garage. He loves to eat; my grocery bill would put the fear of G-d in you. Unless you have boys and can't feel my pain. That tall, bulky skater still hugs his mama and does loving, sweet, and thoughtful things. Then he buys stupid things to put on his car that I don't understand. He calls me *cuzo* and *homey*, which I take to be terms of endearment. I respond, "What's up, pimp?" which makes it immediately weird, but that's how the cool kids talk, or so I'm told, and I'm one of the cool kids. There is this amazing sensitive kindness I hope he never loses. He is pretty darn cute too.

Jackson has grown taller than me as well. Sweet little Jackson. He likes to fish and then come home and spend hours telling me about lures and rods, and I listen and shake my head like it's the coolest thing. I'm sure there's a sex joke in there that we're both thinking but not saying. I like to fish, too, but bringing home a fish doesn't excite me. Now, if we could fish in a sea of Louis Vuitton bags, I'd start telling you about lures and rods too.

Jackson wants to build a barndominium with a giant trampoline inside. I hope he never loses that childlike desire to jump up and down and flip head over foot. Sometimes I go out and jump on the trampoline with him and his friends, which is loads of fun, but I am constantly worried my boob will fall out of my bra in front of them all. Not that I'd be embarrassed, exactly, but I'd rather not have parents calling me up later.

Thoughtful, adorable Jackson worries all the time that I'm okay, and I tell him I'm great and things are fine. When I drop him off for eighth grade, he gives me a hug and kiss, right in front of his friends. His principal saw him and told him to never stop that, and he said, "I won't." I believe him. He thinks differently, and I believe this will lead to great success.

Reese flies planes. What an amazing girl. She goes to the University of North Dakota to pursue a career in commercial aviation. She's an amazing pilot, which is a miracle because she is a crappy driver. As long as she can always get from point A to point B by air, she'll be fine. When she got her private pilot's license a few years back, she asked me to be her first passenger. I said, "Okay, we go up, and we come right back down." I was so scared, I couldn't stop talking the entire time, but she was really quite good at it. We stayed up for forty-five minutes. We flew over farm fields and saw one with a big wedding proposal cut into it. I wanted to go down there and write, *Get a duplex first, you dumbass, so it'll last longer* in cornstalks or something.

Reese is smart, beautiful, and ambitious, and I really miss her. I was hard on her growing up. She was my first and I'd been so worried about her, but she turned out fabulous. Watch for her. She will show up all over the world, speaking multiple languages and taking great photos. If you're lucky, she may even call you her friend.

All three of my kids tease me that as I get older, I'll start looking like a Tyrannosaurus rex with teeny tiny arms. I try to tell them that when we age and get osteoporosis, we shrink in height but not arm length, but they're convinced I have short arms and will look ridiculous. Thanks, kids. Or whatever TikTok video put that weird idea in your head. Guess what? If I develop tyrannosaurus arms when I'm older, I'm going to be thrilled because I'll still be alive.

When I started this book, I was still sad about our old dog dying. Now we have Walter, a 155-pound English mastiff–Great Dane mix who is lazier than anything I've ever encountered. He hates toys, loves bully sticks and filet mignon, and thinks he's the world's largest lap dog. I call him names and complain about him all day, but he ignores it all because he knows I love him and he brings me joy.

I still have my welded tractor and my camera, which I pull out once in a while to play with. I still have amazing friendships—you know who you are. Near and far, from high school to my career, I have met some truly fabulous people. I love you all for all your gifts and your love and support. Thank you for letting me be part of your life too.

One of my dreams come true is the incredible, supportive, loving man I'm with. Yes, my fifty-and-a-half-point man. He adores me. Like, I am his queen. He buys me cards and flowers for no reason. He likes to listen to me talk (and I talk a lot), and I know he's listening because he responds with intelligent things that relate to what I'm saying. He thinks I'm really smart (I happen to think that's a smart thing to think). Most importantly, he is always here for me and the kids during the good, the bad, and the ugly. Except when he goes home. We don't have a duplex, yet, but we live apart with no plans to marry. When people ask if we're married, I say, "No. We're happy." Guess there's still some bitterness there from the divorce.

This man, Keith, makes me feel like a princess. He once gave me a birthday gift straight out of the movies. Keith, my kids, and I were in New York for just a day, and Keith said we needed to be in Times Square at a specific time. When we got there, I looked around for a billboard or sign that would suddenly say, "Happy birthday, Cindy!" or something. It was bittersweet, because one of my regrets was never moving to New York and trying to have a career as a dancer or choreographer on Broadway. To keep his surprise a secret, Keith said that he needed to buy something at the Walgreens on the corner of Seventh Avenue and Broadway. Suddenly, there was music, and a flash mob formed and began dancing in the street. One of the dancers came right up to me and pulled me in, and I realized what was going on. Keith knew we'd be here, knew of my one regret, and he found a way to give me the gift of dancing on Broadway. After the dancers completed two songs, Keith and I danced the third song together, surrounded by these talented performers. I don't think anyone could top that in a million years. (I don't want to speak for Keith, but, ladies, he's very happy with our arrangement, so don't get any ideas or I will send Ari after you. Find your own Prince Charming. There have to be a couple more out there.)

My ex married a woman who speaks only Spanish and lives in Colombia. He sends large payments to her but doesn't keep current on his child support. I still have to go to court over this guy. He barely shows up to see his kids, and when he does, he feeds them McDonald's, which is maybe one step up from a Lunchables. So now my kids have a stepmom they've never met and are eating diabetes every other weekend. People think I'm joking about my divorced women's anthology (remember *My Douchebag Is Bigger Than Your Douchebag?*), but this guy has given me enough to fill the whole volume myself. But he doesn't deserve to be the only one in there, so I've started a list of women who want to contribute.

Walking through cancer convinced me I had to step out of my comfort zone more often. So I signed up for a Tough Mudder race. This was not the smartest choice for me since I hate running, I hate getting muddy, and I hate obstacles. I guess I saw the ad at the right time and wasn't thinking about what it would entail. I knew I needed to get back to exercising, and signing up for something seemed like a good incentive.

Chemo damaged my lungs; I'm at about 76 percent capacity and have Raynaud's now too. If I climb a huge flight of stairs, it will wind me, but I'll tough it out and not complain about it to you. I purchased a hyperbaric oxygen chamber that I slept in every night for a while. It has helped tremendously with the Raynaud's, so I can get through winter with minimal pain. It is now in my practice so others can benefit from it too.

The race was in Lake Geneva, a resort town just over the Wisconsin border. It was a cold, rainy day, miserable and amazing. I had found some other women to sign up with me, and they'd found a few more to fill out the team, so I knew some of the people well, a few only a little, and one not at all. We all started together, but eventually some got way ahead while I fell behind. Kris (a different Kris, though still a good friend, yet I don't know if I have ever eaten her potato salad) and Michelle stayed with me, running when I ran, walking when I had to walk. The obstacles could be difficult in the mud, but you felt a real accomplishment completing them. Strangers helped me walk a slippery balance beam, and I'm sure I pushed a butt or two over the top of a couple walls. The course ended with a slide into a puddle of mud; the three of us went down it together, then walked off the course holding hands. I started to cry; I was so full of gratitude at being alive and being able to do something like that and to have my friends right there with me.

And it was like my walk through cancer. Some people who start with you eventually run ahead. Some will not be around at the end. And a couple will be there with you through the whole thing. That's life, and it's okay. Cancer was another obstacle, or a whole six-month obstacle course, and running it was hard, frustrating, sometimes dirty and wet, sometimes cold, but sometimes fun, and I felt strong and grateful at the end.

I was supposed to get CT scans every six months for five years to

make sure the cancer didn't return. I got one. No cancer. I decided to
not have another one. "They" say that if you experience lymphoma,
the sequela twenty years later may be leukemia. I believe that is
much more likely if I continue to radiate healthy tissue by getting CT
scans every six months, so I decided to take my chances by running
my blood labs every six months and listening to my body instead. I
crossed the five-year mark where I can now say I am cured. I will not
contribute to the chance of the sequela by doing something I believe
will increase my chances. By the way, if I do get it, I will conquer it
just as I did Hodgkin's, and I will write a sequel to this book.

I still love my job, even if I've had to learn to do more telehealth
appointments than I ever thought I would. I'm speaking all over the
place, and I'm helping to develop technology in the field of internal/
functional medicine. When this book comes out, I'll use it to schedule
gigs where I can tell my story and educate people about taking charge
of their health and inspire them to have great attitudes. I expect I'll
be giving one of these talks on the Amalfi Coast or in Ravello, Italy, so
book me now before I get too comfortable there.

Somewhere in these early pages I said I had a theory on why doctors
get sick, and now that I'm wrapping things up, I'm ready to explain it
to you. The long and short of it is energy. Now, this concept is simple,
but it may be hard for some of you to really get your head around
it. As a practitioner, I pick up on my patients' energy. Sometimes
a patient sort of resonates, like they're on the same frequency as I
am, and those patients are often great fits. Oftentimes, I can tell if

you're going to get better or not just by the energy you bring into my office. It's not conscious or anything, but there is an energy exchange. When I work with very sick people, I recognize that it affects me, and I have to do extra work to keep myself healthy. It's okay; that's the job. Remember I mentioned I had this theory why we as doctors get sick? Yep, a little weird, but I do think we can pick up all the negative energy from our patients' illnesses and pain if we don't energetically protect ourselves. I envision myself being zipped up in a protective barrier so I am not as exposed to others' negative energy, and I have to limit my time with people or patients who drain me.

Seriously, if there is anything I can do for you, please reach out. I am always taking new patients or new speaking gigs because there is no better high for me than helping people get healthy, be inspired, develop positive attitudes, and have fun. I've got a lot of life left to live, and I'd love to spend some of it with you. Maybe I'll do that one-woman show. I've already got a midlife crisis mantra for when I get to that point: I'll try anything once to say I did it, twice for fun, three times just to make sure.

I mean, if we aren't having fun, then let's just leave. But I'm still having fun. Join me, won't you?

Oh, you wanted to know about the pickle, the cucumber, and the penis. See, they were talking about how bad their lives were. The cucumber says, "My life is terrible! When I get big and hard, they chop me up and put me in a salad."

The pickle says, "That's nothing! When I get big and hard, they stick me in a jar full of vinegar and vacuum-seal me in."

The penis shakes his head and says, "Not even close! My life is the worst. When I get big and hard, they put a rubber tarp on my head, stick me in a dark room, and bang my head against the wall until I throw up and pass out." It truly is all about perspective.

Aren't you glad you waited till the end?

LAST POSTSCRIPT, I PROMISE:

THE STORY OF MY GHOSTWRITER

What is the history of the term *ghostwriter* anyway? What a ridiculous thing, to call the living person who helped give so much of this book its own kind of flesh a "ghost." I have actually seen a ghost. That might sound crazy to you, but you can't convince me otherwise. It didn't offer to help me write my book; I'll tell you that much.

I have seen a ghost, and I have seen Brad, and he's not a ghost, nor invisible nor nonexistent nor even very scary. He was happy to remain a shadowy presence in this book, but I did not do this all on my own, and I like to show appreciation where appreciation is due, so I made him include this section, which I wrote but he worked his magic on.

That was the arrangement. The story is mine, of course. Most of the words are mine too. Brad took my words and my story and made it more magical—even for me. Some of you may want to write a book and may seek an editor or ghostwriter for help, and I think the story of how I met Brad is instructive.

Brad wasn't my first choice; in fact, he was my third choice. (I've told him all this before, by the way.) He turned out to be my best choice. Remember, the first frog you kiss is not always the prince you marry for happily ever after.

I had this collection of journal entries from my cancer journey, and I had a bunch of editors say it wasn't ready for them or they didn't have time for it. Then I put out a call for proposals on LinkedIn ProFinder. I knew I wanted somebody local to Chicago, and I also wanted to work with a woman. I wound up talking to two women and one man.

I loved talking to the first woman. She was a cancer survivor, too, so I figured she would have a lot of empathy and an inside perspective. She was in Chicago and the kind of person I could see becoming best friends with. When she looked over my manuscript, she thought it was awesome and said she would help brush it up for only $800. I couldn't argue with that price.

The second woman was named Cindy, so we had a fun thing in common there. She worked for a speakers bureau, so I thought she might also be a good connection for speaking gigs. We spoke on the phone, and then she sent me a proposal without even asking to see the manuscript. She wanted something like $36,000 to write the book. I'm not saying she wasn't worth it, but it wasn't what I thought I was getting into. It wasn't like we were starting from scratch, and she hadn't even looked at it to know what it would need or if she'd even want to work on it.

Then I spoke to Brad. Brad wasn't a woman or a cancer survivor—not his fault, but not what I was looking for. Nor did I think we were going to be best friends. But he asked to see part of the manuscript so he could show me what he would do with it. I sent him a couple thousand words and figured, what the hell, give him a shot at it. A couple days later, I saw the email with the attached sample.

I was so nervous to open that email and see what he had written. Would I like it? Would it feel like my story anymore? Had he totally changed it beyond recognition?

I opened the file and began to read it out loud. When I heard what he did with my words, how he had taken my story and pulled out the drama and beauty and snarkiness, the way he made me sound like someone who was writing a book, I started to cry. That's when I knew he was the one. Not a best friend, not a professional contact, but someone with whom I could connect at this intimate level of words. He knew what I was trying to portray without changing my story or changing the emotion, yet putting it into a form I could be proud to publish with my name on it. And now his name is part of it too. If you want help putting your story or idea into words, I will highly recommend Brad Fruhauff to you. You can find him at bradfruhauff.com, where he's got some stuff about writing and some stuff about beer.

Thank you, Brad, for staying true to me and for being another man in my life who can bring me to tears in a very good and healthy way. You will be invited to my twenty-five-year cancer-free picnic if I decide to throw one along with all those who shared in my story. What kind of potato salad will you bring?

ACKNOWLEDGMENTS

"Thank you" was one of the first phrases I taught my kids to say. One of them said these words even before "Mom." It's a simple lesson but an important one, because I believe everyone should use good manners. The world would be a better place if we did.

So bear with me as I have a lot of people to thank. Every character in this memoir played an important role, so instead of listing them all (because that would take another chapter), let me tell you their first names are real (ironically, even Karen). Without characters, there is no story, and without every single one of them, my future would have been carved out differently. I am grateful for all of them. Some characters are still in my life; some have moved on, and both of those circumstances are brilliantly perfect.

After I completed treatment for Hodgkin's lymphoma, which I now refer to as "the speed bump," there were many people in my life who helped me check the box that said "Write a book."

I like to tell everyone that my plan is to buy a jet someday. My daughter, Reese, will be our private pilot (yes, she has the training!), and my team and I will travel the world so I can speak and inspire audiences, and we can grow together with the book's message front and center. There will be enough seats on the plane for everyone who wants to join me. In the meantime, I want to thank those who will be invited.

My kids get a huge thanks and a "big-ass hug" (as my friend Wendy would say). In between all their activities, I have crammed hours of work—sometimes even during their activities. They get it. My relationship with them is fantastic, and I am not just saying that so I look like a great mom. (I am not fantastic on the days when the cramming happens.) But I have worked very hard on balance, communication, and parenting Reese, Ari, and Jackson. They are, after all, my greatest accomplishments. You would be better for knowing them or having late-night conversations about normal stuff with them, like I get to. I will always love you three! A big shout-out to our dog, Walter, too!

I want to share my appreciation for my mom and dad, who have given me everything they knew how to and loved me every day since the moment I existed. I am the best parts of both of them, and their love and support have taught me to keep on keepin' on while telling bad jokes and pursuing my goals. Thanks to my sister, Lisa, who is and will always be supportive of my journey and filled with love for me and my children.

I have to give a big, huge thank-you to my boyfriend, Keith. He was not in my life when I walked through this journey, but he certainly is walking with me now and encouraging me to get the book done, which has taken quite a few years. He even wrote a check for five thousand dollars to help with expenses, since I was initially a little shy about spending so much money to achieve this enormous project. I ripped up the check because I wanted to do this myself, but the message of support was loud and clear, and he continues to support every one of my crazy endeavors. I love you.

Thank you to Brad Fruhauff, who helped me keep my words and brought me to tears when I read them over and over. Kathy Mills Chang, thank you for thinking of Johann Marron Stefan. His team built my brand and taught me that sometimes you have to pick what you need and not always what you love. He and Maria Contreras held my hand and put up with me when I thought I knew more artistically, but I have come to learn there is a reason they are the professionals, and I like to scribble. Thank you to Janet Jerde, who launched my social media efforts and, quite frankly, wears the coolest glasses out of my entire team. A special thanks to T. J. Neathery and Matt Weeden for enabling me to connect with my readers online. I'm grateful for their expertise and helping me invite and welcome new friends to the Dr. Cindy community. And a big thanks to Megan McMullin, who has shown me how to creatively reach new readers who share my passion for living life on your own terms.

Jay Greenstein, your introductions led me to Marissa Eigenbrood, and she is a bright spot on this journey. She pointed the way to many terrific people in the publishing business—from Mari Kesselring, who held my hand, and Tegan Tigani, who created exceptional clarity on the page, to Katherine Richards, who checked my grammar, my facts, and my double-spacing after periods. When did they change that from two spaces to one? And a hearty thanks to Christina Henry de Tessan, who introduced me to her publishing world.

A big visual thank-you to Jay Peters and Greg Owens, who worked on photos and videos. Greg controls my frizzy hair gone wild, and Jay listens to me complain about how women prefer photos from above so we look skinnier. They produce brilliant imagery. Crissy, thank you for the makeup at my first shoot, and Danny at Sephora, your help for round two was a hit. I know you normally do drag makeup, but I asked you for "simple" and you nailed it.

Tony Steck, you designed a beautiful book cover, and you're the second life-saving Tony on my journey. The first one made me radioactive, and you made my cover shine. After many failed attempts, you nailed it for me, so much so that it was difficult to choose which option I liked best.

I'm ever so grateful to everyone who wrote testimonials for me; your words touched my heart. Stephanie Halloran, your reaction to my book inspired me to share it with others. Thank you for writing the foreword and showing me how my story can have a real impact.

I want to thank my fourth-grade teacher, Mrs. Blumenthal at Wescott Elementary, who let me pick Andy Gibb as the subject for my biography essay, while everyone else chose people like Abraham Lincoln. She taught me that you can do what you want and still participate in the activity without apologizing for who you are. Others made fun of my choice, but I didn't care. Andy Gibb was gorgeous, and his pictures kept me interested in the material. Abe Lincoln was not my type. I credit Andy for the good grade I earned.

Thank you to all the doctors, nurses, and staff who work every day to help people get over their challenges and who helped me even in moments when I wasn't sure how to help myself. Thank you for challenging me, Dr. Block, even if I didn't always follow your advice. It was my health and my body, and I got it right.

I want to thank myself for being brave enough to be vulnerable to all of you. It really is true: If this book changes one life for the better, then it will all have been worth it. The expense, the time, and the sleepless nights mulling over book-cover designs were all worth it.

Lastly, but essentially, is Denise McMahan. Marissa Eigenbrood recommended her, and originally I thought, *Wow, she is going to write some blogs for me so I don't have to and because I hate doing that stuff.* Well, Denise is so much more than a writer; I've given her the title of book manager. She never asked for it, but she deserves it. She handles everything. She's on all my calls, writes content, vets other partners, listens to my "crazy," and has supported every decision I have made along the way, which was easy since we tend to think alike. If you are on a journey to write, speak, and dream, then you need Denise. Without her, this book would be less. With her, it has been positively altered.

Acknowledgments wouldn't be complete without you, dear reader. Thank you for reading or listening to my book. I hope it's changed you in positive ways and inspired you to share it with someone else.

Don't forget to thank those who are important to you. It is powerful and life changing.

XO,
Cindy
DrCindySpeaks.com

ABOUT THE AUTHOR

Dr. Cindy M. Howard won the parent lottery with an adoring mother and father who helped with school projects, Halloween costumes, and bad boyfriends and who had an outlook on life that fed Cindy's quick wit.

She spent her youth at two opposite ends of the athletic spectrum: participating in professional dancing, thanks to hours of watching *Solid Gold*, and competitive powerlifting, winning titles in both bench press and dead lift. (Cindy's gym was located in the middle of a cemetery. We'll let you work out the irony between the dead-lift title and the gravestones.)

Today, Cindy excels as a board-certified chiropractic internist and nutritionist, running her own successful practice. She keeps a packed schedule, treating pediatric patients, professional athletes, and everyone in between with conditions ranging from fatigue to autoimmune disease.

Cindy diagnosed herself with Hodgkin's lymphoma, and that soon became the test for what she has always believed: We get to choose how we approach our lives, how we react to what the universe throws at us. Her new book, *Positively Altered*, celebrates this belief system.

Cindy likes to test her humor at home with her kids. They like to say she's "so not funny that it makes her funny," which is confusing, because doesn't that mean she *is* funny?

When Cindy's not seeing patients or speaking onstage, she's navigating life in the South Suburbs of Chicago with her boyfriend, Keith, and her three amazing kids.

Visit www.drcindyspeaks.com to book Dr. Cindy for your next event.

Loved the book?

Then share the laughs in person!
Schedule Dr. Cindy for your next event.

Dr. Cindy's no stranger to wowing audiences. For more than 15 years, Dr. Cindy has left a wake of smiles down the audience aisles.

She's spoken to tens of thousands of people—from intimate groups, where she's facilitating discussions, to several thousand people at a time, when she's featured in the "big show."

+++

"Cancer was just the test for something that I've always believed, which is that we get to choose how we approach our lives, how we react to what the universe throws at us. I want to unpack those learning moments with you and your organization."

www.drcindyspeaks.com/contact